Annual Health Reform Update

Sara E. Wilensky, JD, PhD
Department of Health Policy and Management,
Milken Institute School of Public Health,
The George Washington University

Joel B. Teitelbaum, JD, LLM
Department of Health Policy and Management,
Milken Institute School of Public Health,
The George Washington University

JONES & BARTLETT
LEARNING

LEARNING OBJECTIVES

By the end of this text you will be able to:

- Describe previous national health reform attempts
- Understand why national health reform has been difficult to achieve in the United States
- Analyze why national health reform succeeded in 2010 when so many previous attempts had failed
- Understand the key components of the Patient Protection and Affordable Care Act
- Understand the core rulings of multiple U.S. Supreme Court decisions related to the Affordable Care Act
- Evaluate the political climate regarding repealing and replacing the Affordable Care Act, and understand the main features of legislation drafted toward that end
- Describe key issues going forward related to implementation of the Affordable Care Act

▶ Introduction

The Patient Protection and Affordable Care Act of 2010 (generally referred to as the Affordable Care Act, or ACA) is the most monumental piece of U.S. federal health policymaking in nearly 50 years. It reorders not only many aspects of the health insurance and healthcare delivery systems but also longstanding relationships that underpin those systems. Yet beyond the sheer scope and content of the ACA and the policy trade-offs that led to its passage lies another story: its implementation and subsequent effect on the lives of tens of millions of Americans. Implementation of the ACA is an ongoing, dynamic process for the federal government, states, employers, insurers, providers, patients, and others. In addition, there have been and, no doubt, will continue to be state and federal court decisions across the country that alter the trajectory of the law and its implementation.

The vignette in **BOX 1** describes just a few of the competing viewpoints about the ACA and its role in creating a new and potentially more equitable health insurance system. As ACA implementation moves forward, bear in mind the many different ways that this round of health reform can be perceived and how it affects people differently.

Furthermore, the future of the ACA was made even more uncertain by the monumental election cycle in 2016. Unexpectedly, Donald Trump was elected president in November of that year, and the Republicans maintained control of both the U.S. House of Representatives and the Senate. Having control of Congress and the White House gives Republicans a chance to fulfill a promise they have campaigned on for years—to repeal and replace the ACA. Even if they are not successful in passing a repeal and replacement bill, President Trump can use his executive powers to rewrite existing regulations and implement new policies. Indeed, he has already started to do so, as will be discussed in this text.

The interplay between legal and political decisions makes it difficult to discern how implementation of the law will be carried out, assuming it is not

---

BOX 1 Vignette

A group of friends were talking about the ACA, illustrating the wide-ranging viewpoints about the law. Katherine, whose friend Sophia is struggling to make a living as an artist, is pleased that Sophia has health insurance for the first time since graduating from college. Although Sophia cannot stay on her parents' insurance because she just turned 27 years old, she can now afford a good health insurance plan that she found on her state's health exchange. While Katherine has not noticed much of a change in her own health insurance coverage, which she obtains through her government employer, her cousin Mia is upset about health reform. She does not want the government forcing her to purchase health insurance (although she always chose to be insured in the past), and she recently found out that her old plan was cancelled because it did not meet the law's requirements. Mia found several new plan options to choose from, but none had her former plan's exact combination of benefits, providers, and price. In addition, Katherine's uncle, Ethan, is 55 years old and self-employed. He purchases his health insurance on his state's exchange and because he has preexisting conditions, he is grateful to be able to find a plan. Even so, Ethan's premiums will increase by 15% this year and his deductible is $5,000, making health care difficult to afford even with insurance. Katherine's husband, Calvin, thinks we should all be willing to pay a little more or change some aspects of our plans to help the millions of people who can now afford insurance for the first time as a result of the ACA. After witnessing her uncle's experience, however, Katherine is doubtful that the government will be able to keep its promises.

---

repealed entirely. By way of example, the U.S. Supreme Court's landmark 2012 decision upholding the constitutionality of the ACA and 2015 decision upholding subsidies provided through the ACA to the federal insurance exchange are described in the pages that follow, and there are currently dozens of lawsuits challenging the ACA's coverage mandate related to contraceptive and other family planning services. The practical consequences and legal rulings that actually manifest as a result of ACA implementation—not just the changes to American health care contemplated by Congress when they put pen to paper with the ACA—will, for years to come, need to be studied and understood by students across a range of disciplines, not just for academic purposes, but for healthcare and public health job market purposes as well.

Although there has been general agreement about the problems facing the U.S. healthcare system—high costs, high uninsured rates, health disparities, quality concerns—politicians and voters have disagreed about the best solutions. As a result, numerous attempts to pass national health reform legislation did not succeed. What was different in 2010? Why was the Obama administration successful when several previous attempts had failed? This text begins with a discussion of why it has been so difficult to achieve broad health reform in this country and then examines the numerous failed attempts at national health reform over the last century. It then analyzes how health reform was enacted in 2010, provides an overview of the law that eventually emerged, and covers the U.S. Supreme Court decision upholding its constitutionality. Finally, the discussion turns to the current political climate and what it means for health reform going forward, including a discussion of key political and implementation issues. Throughout this text we examine several key themes: choosing between state flexibility and national uniformity; determining the appropriate role for government, the private sector, and the healthcare financing and delivery entities; defining a primary decision-making goal (e.g., fiscal restraint, equity/social justice, improved health outcomes, uniformity); and settling on the appropriate scope of coverage to offer beneficiaries.

▶ Difficulty Achieving Health Reform in the United States

The array of problems facing the healthcare system has led to numerous health reform proposals and implemented policies. The concept of health reform can have several different meanings. Given the patchwork health insurance system, health reform often refers to changes that seek to reduce the number of uninsured. Due to the high and increasing cost of healthcare services, health reform might also include changes that seek to contain costs and control utilization. The notion of health reform could also address other shortcomings, such as trying to reduce medical errors, strengthening patient rights, building the public health infrastructure, and confronting the rising cost of medical malpractice insurance. Unsurprisingly, the ACA touches on many of these issues.

We begin with a discussion about why health reform is difficult to achieve in the United States and then introduce some of the reforms that have been attempted, with varying degrees of success, on a national level. Numerous authors have addressed the main factors that deter significant social reform in this country, including health reform (Blake & Adolino, 2001; Gordon, 2003; Jost, 2004). Factors that are prominently discussed include the country's culture, the nature of U.S. political institutions, the power of interest groups, and path dependency (i.e., the notion that people are generally opposed to change).

Culture

This country's culture and lack of consensus about health reform have impeded attempts to create universal coverage health plans. The twin concepts of entrepreneurialism and individualism have had a real impact on health policy decisions: Americans generally oppose government solutions to social welfare problems (Jost, 2004, p. 238). In addition, there is no agreement about the overall scope of the healthcare problems we face (Kaiser Family Foundation [KFF], 2008). Prior to the passage of the ACA, most Americans believed the extant health system needed major changes, yet 22% believed only minor changes were required and another 17% thought the system should basically stay the same (KFF, 2009b).

Americans have a complicated and partisan view of the proper role of the federal government in the healthcare arena. On one hand, 60% of respondents to a 2017 survey felt that the federal government has a responsibility to ensure healthcare coverage for all Americans (Kiley, 2017). This is much higher than the 47% who shared that view in 2010, at the height of the health reform debate (Newport, 2010).

Of those who supported federal intervention in the 2017 survey, 33% reported they would like to see a single-payer system developed (Kiley, 2017).

At the same time, there was a stark difference of opinion based on the respondents' political views. While 85% of Democrats and Democrat-leaning independents believed the federal government was responsible for ensuring healthcare coverage, only 32% of Republicans and Republican-leaning independents agreed (Kiley, 2017). Even so, over half (57%) of Republican/Republican-leaners supported the continuation of Medicaid and Medicare, the country's largest public health insurance programs. Furthermore, only 5% of respondents thought the federal government should not have any role in ensuring healthcare coverage (Kiley, 2017).

It is accepted political dogma that it is difficult to take away benefits once they are established, and this has proven to be true with healthcare coverage (Steinhauer, 2017). The popularity of the ACA has increased since the Republicans gained power in the 2016 elections and the threat of repealing the ACA became a realistic possibility. A June 2017 Kaiser Tracking poll showed the ACA's favorability ratings above 50% for the first time since the poll began in 2010 (KFF, 2017b), and a separate poll taken a couple months later showed 64% of respondents preferred to either keep the ACA as it is or make fixes to it that would shore up problems and weaknesses (Kahn & Erman, 2017). Furthermore, the public is clearly opposed to the proposed Republican replacement plans. A majority of respondents opposed both the House (56% opposed) (Magness, 2017) and Senate (55% opposed) (Wynn, 2017) bills. Even though many Republicans also opposed the replacement options (only 21% have a very favorable view) (KFF, 2017b), most Republicans (about 75%) would still like to see the ACA repealed and replaced at some point (Kahn & Erman, 2017).

U.S. Political System

The country's system of government also has made it difficult to achieve universal coverage. Traditionally, social welfare programs—including the provision of health care—have been the responsibility of the states. Initially, there was almost no federal involvement in the provision of health care, and when the federal government became more heavily involved in 1965, Medicaid continued to keep the locus of decision making at the state level. Of course, there are select populations, such as older adults (Medicare) and veterans (Veterans Health Administration), who have a federalized health insurance system. However, support for federal involvement in health care depends on what language is used to describe the change. For example, "single-payer" or "socialized" health care was backed by less than half of the public in a 2017 poll, while "universal health coverage" and "Medicare-for-all" was supported by over 60% (Kaiser Family Foundation [KFF], n.d.(a)).

Although states are generally home to social welfare changes, it is difficult to provide universal health care on a state-by-state basis. If state health reform efforts lead the way, the country could have a patchwork of programs and policies that vary from state to state, with the potential to make health coverage even more complex and inefficient than it is currently. In addition, states must consider whether they are making policy decisions that will give employers an incentive to choose to locate in another state with fewer or less onerous legal requirements. If employers leave the state, it could result in loss of jobs and have downstream effects on the state's economy.

The federal government also has resource advantages over states, making it easier for the federal level to be the engine for health reform. Individual states have a much smaller tax and revenue base than the federal government to draw from to implement health reform plans. In addition, once the federal government decides to tax a good or service, a state's ability to tax that same good or service is constrained by the individual's willingness and ability to pay a higher price. Unlike the federal government, most states have some type of balanced budget requirement (Garrett, 2011). While state legislatures may use accounting gimmicks and other maneuvers to avoid balanced budget requirements, states more often must make difficult choices about resource allocation that federal policymakers often avoid (and thus generate enormous deficits). These restrictions, however, also may help with reform efforts by forcing states to a crisis point where a decision must be made to avoid an untenable situation. The federal government rarely reaches such a crisis point, which means tough decisions are often left for the next Congress, executive branch administration, or generation.

State reform efforts are also constrained by the Employee Retirement Income Security Act of 1974 (ERISA). ERISA is a federal law that regulates "welfare benefit programs," including health plans, operated by private employers. ERISA limits ability of states to reform because it broadly preempts state laws that "relate to" employer-sponsored plans and because it applies to nearly all individuals who receive health benefits through a private employer. One effect of the law, for example, is that states have little regulatory control over the benefits covered in employer-sponsored health plans, because ERISA accords employers near-total discretion over the design of their benefit packages (Weissert & Weissert, 2002, p. 237).

Despite these hurdles, it is also important to recognize that a health reform strategy focusing on states has benefits as well. At its best, reform at the state level can be accomplished more rapidly and with more innovation than at the federal level. State legislatures may have an easier time convincing a narrower band of constituents important to the state than Congress has in accommodating the varied needs of stakeholders nationwide. Along the same lines, states are able to target reforms to meet the particular needs of their population, instead of covering more diverse needs across the entire country. Additionally, through the use of "direct democracy" (e.g., referenda, ballot initiatives), it is easier for citizens to have an impact on decisions by state-level policymakers than by federal legislators. Finally, because the healthcare delivery system is run primarily on the state level, states have the expertise and ability to implement many parts of healthcare reform.

Other aspects of the U.S. political system also make it difficult to institute sweeping reform. For example, although presidents have significant influence on setting policy agenda and proposing budgets, they have limited power to make changes without the assistance of Congress. The federal government is often politically divided, with different parties holding power in the executive and legislative branches. This division often results in partisanship and policy inaction due to different policy priorities and views.

Furthermore, although members of Congress may ride the coattails of a popular president from their own party, they are not reliant on the president to keep their jobs. The issues and views their constituents care about most may not align with the president's priorities. In those cases, members of Congress have a strong incentive to adhere to the wishes of those who vote for them, instead of simply following the president's lead. Barring an overwhelming wave of discontent, as occurred in the 2010 midterm elections when Democrats suffered historic losses in Congress, it is usually difficult to unseat incumbents. Even when there is a historic level of turnover, reelection rates remain very high. For example, 97% of House incumbents successfully defended their seats in 2016; even in the Senate, where turnover is relatively more common, 93% of incumbents won reelection in 2016 (Kondick & Skelley, 2016). As a result, legislators in Congress may have confidence in focusing on their district's or state's needs before those of the entire nation.

Federal legislative rules also support inaction or incremental reform over sweeping changes. In the Senate, 60 (of 100) votes are needed to break a filibuster in most cases. Thus, even the political party in the majority can have difficulty effecting change. One exception to the filibuster rule is the "reconciliation" process, which allows bills to pass with only 51 votes. Reconciliation is used as part of the budgetary process, and bills passed via reconciliation may not be filibustered (so can pass with 51 votes), can pertain only to federal revenue and spending issues, must comply with spending and revenue targets set forth in the budget resolution, and must adhere to other budgetary rules (Tax Policy Center, n.d.). The reconciliation process is being increasingly used when one party maintains a slim majority and that party cannot find 60 votes to pass a bill. For example, the Democrats used a reconciliation bill to pass the ACA in 2010 after they lost their filibuster-proof majority, and likewise, the Republicans attempted to use a reconciliation bill to pass their ACA repeal-and-replace bills. Also, because both the House and the Senate have to pass bills containing the same policies and language to have any chance at becoming law, a large political majority in one chamber or the other does not guarantee the ability to enact a policy. As a result, in many cases members of Congress have to work together, at least to some degree, to devise a consensus policy that satisfies enough members to pass a bill. This need to build consensus makes radical change unlikely.

Interest Groups

Interest groups often influence the decisions of politicians. The role of interest groups is to represent their members' interests in policy decisions. These groups can be corporate for-profit entities or nonprofit consumer-oriented organizations. They lobby politicians and the general public about the virtues or vices of specific proposals, work to improve proposals on the policy agenda, and attempt to defeat proposals they believe are not in the best interest of their group. By contributing to political campaigns or by helping to draw supportive voters out on Election Day, interest groups gain the ear, and often the influence, of politicians who vote on issues that are important to the group.

In terms of health reform, interest groups representing various providers, businesses, employer groups, insurance companies, and managed care organizations often have been opposed to comprehensive health reform (Jost, 2004, pp. 438–439). There are numerous points along the path—from developing a policy idea to voting for or against a bill—when interest groups can attempt to affect politicians' views.

The more radical the policy proposal, the more interest groups are likely to become engaged in the political decision-making process, making it difficult to pass a bill that includes comprehensive reform.

In general, it is easier to oppose a proposal than to develop one and pass a bill. Opponents of proposals are not required to provide a better alternative to whatever is on the table. Instead, they can simply point to aspects of the policy idea that are unpopular and call for the proposal to be rejected. This was the tactic used by the Health Insurance Association of America in their well-known "Harry and Louise" television ads that opposed the Clinton administration's comprehensive health reform bill in 1993, the Health Security Act. In the ad, Harry and Louise, two "average" Americans, are seen discussing the healthcare system over break-fast. Although they both agree the system needs to be improved, they highlight certain aspects of the Clinton plan that were particularly controversial, such as an overall cap on funds for healthcare needs and restrictions on provider choice. The tag line for the ad was, "There's got to be a better way" (West, Heith, & Goodwin, 1996). Similarly, before the 2016 elections, many Republicans promised to "repeal and replace" the health reform bill without specifying their favored replacement option. To be effective in opposing health reform, opponents did not have to pro-pose an alternative that was scrutinized and compared with the existing proposal. Simply saying "the country can do better" was enough to help create significant opposition to the plan.

Path Dependency

Finally, the concept of path dependency has been a hindrance to major health reform. "The notion of path dependency emphasizes the power of inertia within political institutions" (Jost, 2004, p. 439). That is, once a certain way of doing things becomes the norm, it is hard to change course. Yet this theory does not mean that health reform is impossible. Inertia may be overcome at "critical moments or junc-tures" that open a window for change (Jost, 2004, p. 439). For example, the passage of Medicaid and Medicare in 1965 was a radical change from the past pattern of limited federal government involvement in health care. The catalysts for this change were the growing social pressure for improving the healthcare system and the land-slide victory of Democrat Lyndon Johnson as president and of liberal and moderate Democrats in Congress.

The 1992 election of Democrat Bill Clinton, who ran on a platform emphasiz-ing broad health reform, coupled with the Democratic majority in Congress (until 1994), also presented a window of opportunity. Although Clinton's plan was not ulti-mately successful, it appeared that the American public and politicians were open to changing the course of the healthcare "path" that had been taken to date. In 2010 another "critical moment" appeared, and President Obama took advantage of the circumstances to push through the health reform bill. Although path dependency suggests that inertia and fear of change have made broad reform difficult, it is not impossible to achieve.

Path dependency is also evident on the individual level; that is, once indi-viduals are accustomed to having things a certain way, it is difficult for them to accept change. In 2010, prior to the passage of the ACA, about 84% of Americans had health insurance, most through employer-sponsored coverage (U.S. Census Bureau [Census], 2010). It was assumed that comprehensive health reform would likely change the condition of the insured population to some degree by changing either their source of coverage, the benefits included in coverage, the cost of coverage, or some other factor. During the debate over the ACA, about one-third of people surveyed reported that the bill would probably make them worse off, and another third thought it would not make any difference to them (KFF, 2008). Professor Judith Feder refers to this problem as the "crowd-out" politics of health reform: "The fundamental barrier to universal coverage is that our success in insuring most of the nation's population has 'crowded out' our political capacity to insure the rest" (Feder, 2004, p. 461). In other words, many of the insured do not want a change in the healthcare system that will leave them worse off to make the uninsured better off.

According to Professor Feder, the way to solve the political crowd-out dilemma is by changing the very nature of American culture. The focus on individualism must be replaced with a concern for the community and recognition that all Americans are part of a single community. "The challenge to improving or achieving universal coverage is to decide whether we are a society in which it is every man, woman or child for him/herself or one in which we are all in it together" (Feder, 2004, p. 464). Clearly, the country remains divided about the extent to which "we are all in it together." Shortly before the ACA passed, over half of people surveyed (54%) said they would not be willing to pay more so others could have access to health insurance (KFF, 2009a). The continued debate over the future of the ACA has highlighted fundamental disagreements about how our health system should be structured and the proper role of individuals and governments in ensuring the country's good health.

▶ Unsuccessful Attempts to Pass National Health Insurance Reform

Since the early 1900s, when medical knowledge became advanced enough to make health care and health insurance desirable commodities, there have been periodic attempts to implement universal coverage through national health reform. The Socialist Party was the first U.S. political party to support health insurance in 1904, but the main engine behind early efforts for national reform was the American Association for Labor Legislation (AALL), a "social progressive" group that hoped to reform capitalism, not overthrow it (Starr, 1982, p. 243). In 1912, Progressive Party candidate Theodore Roosevelt supported a social insurance platform modeled on the European social insurance tradition that included health insurance, workers' compensation, old-age pensions, and unemployment insurance. After his loss to Woodrow Wilson, the national health insurance movement was without a strong national leader for three decades.

The AALL continued to support a form of health insurance after Roosevelt's defeat and drafted a model bill in 1915. This bill followed the European model, limiting participation to working class employees and their dependents. Benefits included medical aid, sick pay, maternity benefits, and a death benefit. These costs were to be financed by employers, employees, and the state. The AALL believed that health insurance for the working population would reduce poverty and increase society's productivity and well-being through healthier workers and citizens.

Opposition to AALL's bill came from several sources (Starr, 1982, pp. 247–249). Although some members of the American Medical Association (AMA) approved of the bill conceptually, physician support rapidly evaporated when details emerged about aspects of the plan that would negatively impact their income and autonomy. The American Federation of Labor (a labor union) opposed compulsory health insurance because it wanted workers to rely on their own economic strength, not the state, to obtain better wages and benefits. In addition, the federation was concerned that it would lose power if the government, not the union, secured benefits for workers. Employers were generally opposed to the bill, contending that supporting public health was a better way to ensure productivity. In addition, they feared that providing health insurance to employees might promote malingering instead of reducing lost workdays. After experiencing the high cost associated with workers' compensation, employers also were not eager to take on an additional expensive benefit. Of course, the part of the insurance industry that had already established a profitable niche in the death benefit business was strongly opposed to a bill that included a death benefit provision. Employers, healthcare providers, and insurers have, in general, remained staunch opponents of national health reform over the years, whereas unions have supported national reform efforts. However, this dynamic has changed recently with more provider groups, employers, and even some insurers calling for a national solution to the problems of rising healthcare costs and the uninsured.

The country's entry into World War I in 1917 also changed the health reform debate. Many physicians who supported the AALL bill entered the military, shifting their focus away from the domestic health policy debate. Anti-German sentiment was high, so opponents of the bill gained traction by denouncing compulsory health insurance as anti-American. One pamphlet read as follows: "What is Compulsory Social Health Insurance? It is a dangerous device, invented in Germany, announced by the German Emperor from the throne the same year he started plotting and preparing to conquer the world" (Starr, 1982, p. 253).

The next time national health insurance might have taken hold was from the mid-1930s through the early 1940s as the country was coping with the difficulties of the Great Depression. During this time there was a significant increase in government programs, including the creation of Social Security in 1935, which provided old-age assistance, unemployment compensation, and public assistance. Yet the fourth prong of the social insurance package, health insurance, remained elusive. President Franklin Roosevelt heeded his staff's advice to leave health insurance out of Social Security because of the strong opposition it would create (Starr, 1982, p. 267). Opposition from the AMA was particularly strong. The AMA believed that "socialized medicine" would increase bureaucracy, limit physician freedom, and interfere with the doctor–patient relationship.

Even so, members of Roosevelt's administration continued to push for national health insurance. The Interdepartmental Committee to Coordinate Health and Welfare Activities was created in 1935 and took on the task of studying the nation's healthcare needs. This job fell to its Technical Committee on Medical Care. Instead of supporting a federal program, the committee proposed subsidies to the states for operating health programs. Components of the proposal included expanding maternal and child health and public health programs under Social Security, expanding hospital construction, increasing aid for medical care for the indigent, studying a general medical care program, and creating a compensation program for those who lost wages due to disability.

Although President Roosevelt established a National Health Conference to discuss the recommendation, he never fully supported the medical care committee's proposal. With the success of conservatives in the 1938 election and the administration's concerns about fighting the powerful physician and state medical society lobbies, national health reform did not have a place on Roosevelt's priority list. Senator Robert Wagner (D-NY) introduced a bill that followed the committee's recommendations in 1939, and although it passed in the Senate, it did not garner support from the president or from the House.

World War II provided another opportunity for the opposition to label national health insurance as socialized medicine. But once the war neared an end, President Roosevelt finally called for an "economic bill of rights" that included medical care. President Truman picked up where Roosevelt left off, strongly advocating for national health insurance. President Truman's proposal included expanding hospitals, increasing public health and maternal and child health services, providing federal aid for medical research and education, and, for the first time, a single health insurance program for all (Starr, 1982, p. 281). Heeding lessons from earlier reform failures, Truman emphasized that his plan was not socialized medicine and that the delivery system for medical and hospital care would not change.

Again, there was strong opposition to the proposal. The AMA vehemently rejected the proposal, and most other healthcare groups opposed it as well. Although the public initially approved of it, there was no consensus about how national health insurance should be structured, and more people preferred modest voluntary plans over a national, compulsory, comprehensive health insurance program (Starr, 1982, p. 282). Additional opposition came from the American Bar Association, the Chamber of Commerce, and even some federal agencies concerned about losing control over their existing programs. In the end, only the hospital construction portion of the proposal was enacted.

When Truman won reelection on a national health insurance platform in 1948, it appeared the tide had turned. However, the AMA continued its strong opposition and its attempts to link national health insurance to socialism. Congress considered various compromises but never reached a consensus. The public remained uncertain about what kind of plan to favor. Employers maintained their opposition to compulsory insurance. In addition, one large group of potential supporters—veterans— was disinterested in the debate because they had already secured extensive medical coverage through the Veterans Administration. As the Korean War moved forward, Truman's focus shifted away from national health insurance and toward the war effort and other priorities.

National health insurance did not return to the national policy agenda until the 1970s. The landscape then was quite different from Truman's era. Medicaid and Medicare had been created, healthcare costs had begun to rise exponentially, and the economy was deteriorating. In 1969, President Nixon declared that a "massive crisis" existed in health care and that unless it was fixed immediately, the country's medical system would collapse (Starr, 1982, p. 381). The general public seemed to agree, with 75% of respondents in one survey concurring that the healthcare system was in crisis (Starr, 1982, p. 381). Democrats still controlled Congress by a significant margin, and Senator Edward Kennedy (D-MA) and Representative Martha Griffiths

(D-MI), the first woman to serve on the powerful House Committee on Ways and Means, proposed a comprehensive, federally operated health insurance system.

At the same time, a movement supporting health care and patient rights was gaining momentum. This movement included rights to informed consent, to refuse treatment, to due process for involuntary commitment, and to equal access to health care (Starr, 1982, p. 389). The public was both anxious to obtain care and willing to challenge the authority of healthcare providers.

The Nixon administration's first attempt at health reform focused on changing the healthcare system's financing from one dominated by a fee-for-service system, which created incentives to provide more and more expensive services, to one that promoted restraint, efficiency, and the health of the patient. The result was a "health maintenance strategy" intended to stimulate the private industry to create health maintenance organizations (HMOs) through federal planning grants and loan guarantees, with the goal of enrolling 90% of the population in an HMO by the end of the 1970s (Starr, 1982, pp. 395–396). Ironically, group health plans, often labeled socialized medicine, had become the centerpiece of a Republican reform strategy.

Nixon's proposal included an employer mandate to provide a minimum package of benefits under a National Health Insurance Standards Act, a federally administered Family Health Insurance Program for low-income families that had a less generous benefit package than the one required by the National Health Insurance Standards Act, reductions in Medicare spending to help defray the costs, a call for an increase in the supply of physicians, and a change in how medical schools were subsidized. Opponents were plentiful, and this plan did not come to fruition. Some believed the plan was a gift to private insurance companies. Advocates for the poor were outraged at the second tier of benefits for low-income families. The AMA was concerned about HMOs interfering with physician practices and supported an alternative that provided tax credits for buying private insurance.

After the 1972 election, Nixon proposed a second plan that covered everyone and offered more comprehensive coverage. Private insurance companies would cover the employed and a government-run program would cover the rest of the population, with both groups receiving the same benefit package. Senator Kennedy and Representative Wilbur Mills (D-AR) supported a similar plan, and it appeared a compromise was close at hand. However, labor unions and liberal organizations preferred the original Kennedy plan and resisted compromising with the hope of gaining power in the 1974 post-Watergate elections. Fearing the same political shift, insurance companies actually supported a catastrophic insurance plan proposed by Senator Russell Long (D-LA), believing it was better than any plan that would come out of a more liberal Congress after the elections. Once again, there was no majority support for any of the bills, and a national health insurance plan was not enacted.

Although President Jimmy Carter gave lip service to national health reform, he never fully supported a proposal. It was not until the election of Bill Clinton in 1992 that the next real attempt at national health insurance was made. The Clinton administration plan, dubbed the Health Security Act, was designed to create national health insurance without spending new federal funds or shifting coverage from private to public insurance. It relied on the concept of "managed competition," which combined elements of managed care and market competition.

Under the Health Security Act, a National Health Board would have established national and regional spending limits and regulated premium increases. "Health alliances" would have included a variety of plans that were competing for the business of employees and unemployed citizens in each geographic area. All plans were to have a guaranteed scope of benefits and uniform cost-sharing. Employers would have been required to provide coverage for their workers at a defined high level of benefits, and those with 5,000 employees or fewer would have had to purchase plans through the health alliance. Subsidies were provided for low-income individuals and small businesses. Funding was to be provided from cost-containment measures that were reinvested. Forced by the Congressional Budget Office to provide an alternative funding strategy should the cost containment not create enough funds, the plan also included the option of capping insurance premium growth and reducing provider payments.

Like the national health insurance plans before it, the Health Security Act had opponents from many directions. The health alliances were attacked as big government, employers resisted mandates and interference with their fringe benefits, some advocates feared that cost containment would lead to care rationing, the insured were concerned about losing some of their existing benefits or cost-sharing arrangements, older adults feared losing Medicare, and academic health centers were concerned about losing funds based on new graduate medical education provisions (Starr, 1982, p. 463). In addition, the usually strong support from unions was missing because of an earlier disagreement with the president on trade matters. It is also generally accepted that the Clinton administration made several political mistakes that made a difficult political chore nearly impossible. The Health Security Act never made it to a vote.

▶ The Stars Align (Barely): How the ACA Became Law

In many ways, 2010 was a very unlikely year to pass a national health reform plan. The country had been growing increasingly ideological, with the popular and electoral votes almost evenly split in both the 2000 and 2004 presidential elections. George W. Bush beat Al Gore despite losing the popular vote in 2000, and Bush beat John Kerry in 2004 with only 51% of the popular vote. Even though Barack Obama won the electoral vote in a landslide over John McCain (365 to 173), only 53% of the population voted for Obama in 2008 (National Archives and Records Administration, n.d.).

In addition to the ideological divide, a financial crisis erupted toward the end of the 2008 presidential election. In October 2008, President Bush signed into law the Emergency Economic Stabilization Act, which included the $700 billion Troubled Asset Relief Program (TARP) that allowed the federal government to take over distressed assets, primarily bad mortgage loans, from private financial institutions (Emergency Economic Stabilization Act of 2008). It was argued that TARP was necessary to save the financial industry from collapsing, which could have led to another Great Depression. Even with TARP, the United States (and many other countries) entered into a recessionary period. Many individuals lived in homes they could no longer afford, banks limited lending opportunities, and employers laid off millions of workers due to the drop in consumer spending. In an effort to improve the economy, Obama signed into law the American Recovery and Reinvestment Act of 2009, also known as the stimulus bill. This almost $800 billion effort was intended to save existing jobs, create new jobs, and spur long-term growth of the U.S. economy. Although TARP was not popular with politicians or the general public, it was seen as necessary by members of both political parties and signed into law by a Republican president. Unlike TARP, however, the stimulus bill was not a bipartisan effort. Republicans in the House unanimously opposed the stimulus bill, and only three Republicans voted for the bill in the Senate.

Not surprisingly, health care was not the only issue on voters' minds during the election campaign. Shortly before the election, 43% of registered voters ranked the economy as their number one priority. Economic concerns trumped health care, which ranked second, by an almost two-to-one margin (Jones, 2010). Although voters from both political parties ranked the economy as their top priority, differences emerged along party lines regarding the next most important issue. Democratic voters ranked health care second, whereas both Republican and Independent voters were more concerned about the size and power of the federal government. These results were not surprising; Democrats have ranked health care as a higher priority than Republican and Independent voters in every presidential election from 1988 to 2012 (Blendon et al., 2008, p. 2053; Jones, 2010).

It was against this backdrop of a faltering economy, partisan differences, and the recent passage of two massive government spending bills that President Obama pursued a national health reform plan. Given the history of failed reform efforts, it would have been an accomplishment to pass health reform in the best of times, and clearly this was not the best of times. How did Obama and the 111th Congress succeed? It was a combination of having commitment, exhibiting leadership, applying lessons from past failures, and being pragmatic that led to the passage of health reform.

Commitment and Leadership

It is highly unlikely that the 2010 health reform effort would have succeeded without a passionate and committed president willing to make health reform a priority. Health care has long been a priority for Democrats, and President Obama was no exception. Perhaps Obama's dedication to passing health reform stemmed in part from his personal experience: Obama's mother died of ovarian cancer, and he had seen her worry about paying her medical bills as much as beating the disease (Kornreich, 2007). Thus, for Obama, signing comprehensive health reform legislation into law would represent the opportunity to make sure others would not endure the same experience.

Some of Obama's political advisors suggested waiting to tackle health reform until after taking action to address the poor economy and rising unemployment. Even voters who supported Obama were split over what his priorities should be during his first days in office (Appleby, 2008). Just days before the election, Obama suggested that the economy and energy independence were higher priorities than health reform. To Obama, that meant he should tackle several majors issues at once, not put health reform on the back burner.

Health reform efforts did not begin smoothly. President Obama initially wanted former U.S. senator Tom Daschle to run both the Department of Health and Human

Services (HHS) and the White House Office on Health Reform. It was thought that his experience in the Senate and relationships with legislators were the right combination to take the lead on health reform. When his nomination was derailed due to personal tax problems, it was not a good omen. As deliberations in Congress lagged, Democrats were not able to present a bill to President Obama before recessing for the summer. During the summer of 2009, members of Congress went home to their constituents and held town hall meetings to discuss health reform. Some of the meetings erupted in vocal opposition to health reform, and the media focused on these town hall meetings throughout the summer. Obama and the Democrats were criticized for losing the momentum for reform by letting the debate linger.

At the same time, there were several instances when the health reform effort appeared politically doomed, and President Obama's leadership made a clear difference. Obama attempted to reclaim the upper hand on health reform with a speech to a joint session of Congress in September 2009. He memorably proclaimed, "I am not the first president to take up health reform, but I intend to be the last" (White House, 2009b). Although public support for health reform had been on the decline for several months, September 2009 polls showed that 62% still thought it was important to address health reform at that time, and 53% thought the country as a whole would be better off if health reform passed (KFF, 2009c). Less support existed for the Democrats' specific reform proposal, however, with 46% in support of the proposed change and 48% opposed to it (Cohen & Balz, 2009).

In January 2010, an event occurred that some assumed was the death knell of health reform. In the 2008 elections, Democrats had made significant gains in Congress, earning a 59–41 majority in the Senate and a 257–178 majority in the House. Furthermore, Senator Arlen Specter of Pennsylvania switched parties, giving Democrats the crucial 60th vote needed for a filibuster-proof majority. Although the numbers were now in their favor, President Obama, Senate Majority Leader Harry Reid (D-NV), and House Speaker Nancy Pelosi (D-CA) would have to balance the competing interests of conservative Democrats who were concerned with having too much government intervention, progressive Democrats who sought a public insurance option to compete with private companies, Blue Dog Democrats who were most concerned with fiscal discipline, and pro-life and pro-choice factions who would battle over whether and how abortion services would be included in any health reform bill.

Then, in August 2009, Senator Ted Kennedy (D-MA) died. In office for 47 years, Kennedy was not only a lifelong supporter of health reform but also an expert negotiator who could work with Republicans and possibly achieve a bipartisan consensus. The January 2010 special election to fill his seat was won by Republican Scott Brown, who campaigned against the Democrats' health reform plan. In a postelection poll, 42% of voters said they voted for Brown to stop health reform from moving ahead (Condon, 2010).

Despite this setback and concerns by some that health reform efforts should be abandoned, Obama, along with Reid and Pelosi, remained strong in his conviction to pursue reform. President Obama's senior advisors said it would be a "terrible mistake" to walk away from the process based on Brown's victory, and Pelosi reminded her caucus how detrimental it was when Democrats abandoned the health reform effort during the Clinton administration (Brown & O'Connor, 2010). In his State of the Union address just a week after Senator Brown claimed the special election,

President Obama tied his health reform efforts to fixing the economy and reiterated his commitment to the issue:

> And it is precisely to relieve the burden on middle class families that we still need health reform. Now let's be clear, I did not choose to tackle this issue to get some legislative victory under my belt. And by now it should be fairly obvious that I didn't take on health reform because it was good politics.... Here is what I ask of Congress though: Do not walk away from reform. Not now. Not when we are so close. Let us find a way to come together and finish the job for the American people. (White House, 2010)

Obama was not alone in providing leadership on health reform. Reid's and Pelosi's determination to see health reform succeed, and their skill in mobilizing and controlling their caucuses, were essential to the passage of the ACA. It is likely that health reform would not have passed without the skillful efforts of all three leaders working together. Even so, it is clear that the health reform effort would not even have begun without a president who put health reform at the top of the agenda and stuck with it despite the pitfalls and political opposition.

Lessons From Failed Health Reform Efforts

The Obama administration tried to avoid events that doomed earlier health reform efforts. Although the failed effort by the Clinton administration probably provided the most relevant lessons, Obama confronted some of the same obstacles that reformers had faced decades earlier. At times, President Obama was accused of learning some of the lessons too well, swinging the pendulum too far to the other side. Although that debate may continue, clearly the way in which the Obama administration applied those lessons brought him success where others had failed before him.

President Clinton was criticized for not moving quickly enough to try to enact health reform after he was elected in 1992. He did not present a plan to Congress until a year into his presidency, having been sidetracked by other issues such as the economy, including a budget showdown with Republicans, and whether gays should be allowed to serve in the military. Even after he finally sent his healthcare proposal to Congress, Clinton was preoccupied with other issues that sapped his political capital, such as passing the North American Free Trade Agreement and the fallout from the deaths of 18 American soldiers in Somalia.

President Obama, over the objection of some aides, chose to address health reform as quickly as possible, despite also having to tackle the poor economy and possible collapse of the financial sector. Obama was elected into office with a 70% approval rating, and he moved to capitalize on his popularity (Saad, 2008). It was almost inevitable that his approval rating would decline as he tried to turn the promise of a campaign into the reality of running the country. As Lyndon Johnson said after winning the 1964 election in a landslide, "Every day while I'm in office, I'm gonna lose votes" (Blumenthal & Morone, 2009, p. 172). In addition, it is almost universally expected that the president's party will lose seats in the midterm elections due to both lower voter turnout that gives more clout to partisan voters and a loss of popularity as the president moves from candidate to elected official (Wihbey, 2014). Obama was correct to assume his Democratic majorities in Congress would not last long. After the 2010 midterm elections, the Democrats lost control of the House and several seats in the Senate.

President Obama also dealt with interest groups in a different way from his predecessors. Previous failed efforts at health reform have shown that those vested interests can be important players in the debate. In general, though not in all instances, provider groups, insurers, and employers have opposed health reform, whereas unions have supported health reform efforts. All of these stakeholders have been known to devote significant resources and apply pressure on their representatives to support their point of view. During its reform effort, the Clinton administration warred with many stakeholder groups, with insurance companies and small businesses taking a leading role (West & Heith, 1996).

Obama took a different approach than Clinton by making deals with various stakeholders at the outset of the health reform debate. The lure of millions of newly insured customers helped convince the Pharmaceutical Research and Manufacturers of America and the American Hospital Association to contribute to health reform financing through reduced Medicare and Medicaid payments. In addition, the health insurance industry supported universal insurance coverage under health reform. After being credited with helping derail the Clinton health plan, the Health Insurance Association of America favored the general idea of health reform, though it differed with Obama and the Democrats on some of the specifics. To be fair, Clinton may not have been able to broker deals with these stakeholders in the 1990s no matter how hard he tried. A combination of a changing healthcare environment, the likelihood that some type of health reform was likely to pass, and the uncertain future of employer-sponsored insurance made it more palatable for interest groups to try to influence instead of oppose the 2010 legislation (Oberlander, 2010).

Clinton was also criticized for failing to master the legislative process. The Clinton administration chose to design the health reform plan itself and developed a complicated and secretive process, headlined by the Health Care Task Force run by Hillary Clinton, to do so. Although naming Hillary Clinton as the leader of the task force signaled the administration's commitment to the issue, she became a lightning rod for criticism, and questions about the appropriateness of the First Lady taking on such a significant policy role detracted from the substance of the health reform debate. Instead of negotiating with Congress, the administration debated the specifics of health reform among its own advisors and then asked Congress to pass the bill they had developed. Shutting out members of Congress instead of negotiating with them and taking over Congress's role in developing legislation was not, it turned out, a formula for success.

President Obama learned from Clinton's mistakes as well as from other presidents' legislative achievements. Instead of presenting a detailed plan or written legislation to Congress, success has often been found in outlining ideas and principles and letting Congress work through the details. When President Johnson was trying to get a Medicare bill passed, he told key members of Congress that he would not delve into the details of the bill but generally pushed for a larger package. When President George W. Bush was pursuing a new Medicare prescription drug benefit, he outlined his desire for an approach that worked with the private sector and encouraged competition, but let Congress find the exact formula that would pass (Morone, 2010, p. 1097).

Similarly, Obama set out his principles but left the work of drafting a bill and fleshing out the details to Congress. On June 2, 2009, President Obama sent a letter to Senators Kennedy and Baucus, two leaders in the health reform effort, outlining his "core belief" that Americans deserved better and more affordable health insurance choices and that a health reform bill must not add to the federal deficit (White House, 2009a). Although he let the negotiators know what his priorities were, Obama stayed above the fray during the legislative process. Whereas he preferred a public option to compete with private insurers, he did not insist on it. Although Obama campaigned against an individual mandate as a presidential candidate, he was open to including it in the bill. The president refused to be drawn into the debate over taxing generous health plans or creating a Medicare cost-containment commission. Instead, he focused his efforts on persuading Congress not to give up on the effort, bringing together various factions of the Democratic caucus, and reaching out to the public to garner support for health reform.

The legislative process for completing the bill was long, rocky, and ultimately partisan. The House of Representatives moved more quickly and with less fractious debate than the Senate. Instead of having multiple House committees work on competing bills, as occurred during the Clinton administration, House Democratic leaders created a "Tri-Committee" bill jointly sponsored by Charles Rangel (D-NY), Henry Waxman (D-CA), and George Miller (D-CA), the chairmen of the House Ways and Means, Energy and Commerce, and Education and Labor (later renamed the Education and Workforce committee) committees, respectively. On November 7, 2009, the House passed its health reform bill with only two votes to spare, 220–215 (Affordable Health Care for America Act, 2009). Only one Republican voted for it, and 39 conservative Democrats voted against it. The bill from the then-more-liberal House contained several provisions that were likely to be rejected by the Senate: a public health insurance option to compete with private plans, a national health insurance exchange instead of state-based exchanges, more generous subsidies for low-income individuals, a broader expansion of Medicaid, and higher taxes on wealthier Americans.

Finance Committee Chairman Max Baucus (D-MT) led the effort in the Senate. The legislative process he established was lengthy, and some observers believed he compromised on too many issues in an attempt to forge a bipartisan bill. For a time Senator Charles Grassley (R-IA) actively participated in the health reform deliberations, and a few other Republican senators appeared willing to consider a bipartisan measure. Ultimately, however, a bipartisan agreement could not be reached. In a 2009 Christmas Eve vote, the Baucus bill passed 60–39, with all Democrats and two Independents voting for the measure and all Republicans voting against it (ACA, 2010).

Shortly after the New Year, members of the House and Senate began meeting to resolve differences between the bills passed in the House and the Senate. Before those differences were resolved, however, Scott Brown was elected to fill Kennedy's seat in the Senate and the Democrats no longer had a filibuster-proof majority. Before the special election that led to Brown's victory, it was assumed that after the Senate passed a health reform measure, House and Senate negotiators would work out their differences in a conference committee, with each chamber then voting to pass the compromise bill. With Brown's election and his opposition to health reform, however, this plan became unworkable. Democratic congressional leaders were left with few options, all of them unpalatable: the House could pass the Senate version of the bill; Democrats could try to use the reconciliation process—which does not allow for the use of filibusters and requires only a simple majority vote—to pass a new comprehensive bill; the House and Senate could compromise on a much smaller, more incremental health reform bill that focused on areas where a bipartisan agreement could be reached; or Democrats could abandon their efforts to pass a health reform bill. The day after Brown's election, House Speaker Pelosi appeared to eliminate the easiest (legislatively speaking) of these paths by declaring that the House would not pass the Senate version of the bill: "I don't think it's possible to pass the Senate bill in the House. I don't see the votes for it at this time" (Murray & Kane, 2010).

In the end, a compromise was reached. House and Senate leaders agreed to use the budget reconciliation process to amend the Senate bill. The House then passed the Senate version of the bill along with a companion reconciliation bill that amended certain aspects of the Senate bill. The reconciliation bill included more generous subsidies for individuals to purchase insurance than existed in the stand-alone Senate bill, the closure of the Medicare Part D doughnut hole, a tax on more generous insurance plans, changes to the penalties on individuals who would not buy insurance and for employers that would not offer insurance, and an increase in Medicare and investment taxes for higher earners. The Senate then passed the reconciliation bill. Once again, the final vote to approve the bills was along party lines. The House approved the Senate bill by a vote of 219–212, with all Republicans and 34 Democrats voting against it (Khan, 2010). President Obama signed the bill into law on March 23, 2010 (ACA, 2010).

Some observers argue that Obama may have overlearned the lesson about working with Congress and that in doing so he did not provide enough guidance to legislators and allowed the debate over health reform to linger for too long (Morone, 2010, p. 1097). On the one hand, it is difficult to criticize Obama's approach because he was ultimately successful. On the other hand, could the problems stemming from the 2009 town halls and Scott Brown's election have been avoided, and would public opinion of the health reform effort be higher, if the process had been better managed? Only time will tell whether Obama was successful over the long term (e.g., Is the law effective? Will the public support it over time? Will it be repealed?) and whether the political cost of the lengthy battle hurt the Democrats more than passing the bill helped them.

Political Pragmatism

President Obama is both credited and criticized for being as pragmatic as necessary to help ensure that a health reform law came to fruition. He was comfortable making deals with industry stakeholders even though those agreements limited the savings and other changes that could have been achieved in the health reform bill. Obama ultimately signed a bill that did not include a public option, even though he preferred that one be included, and his liberal base thought health reform without such an option was not true reform. An argument over abortion nearly derailed the bill in its final days, and Obama supported a compromise on abortion language to keep enough Democrats in the fold. Even his goal of creating universal insurance coverage was not recognized. Yet Obama's willingness to be pragmatic instead of staunchly principled, taking some victories instead of an all-or-nothing approach, allowed him to succeed in passing a health reform bill where others had failed (Oberlander, 2010, p. 1116). Some people argued it was worse to pass a flawed bill than not pass a bill at all, but Obama believed the promise of reducing the uninsured rate and gaining numerous health insurance market reforms were worth the compromises he made.

▶ Overview of the ACA

As noted earlier, while President Obama left the details of health reform legislation to Congress, he set forth what he believed to be the most important principles that should guide the legislation's development. Soon after becoming president in 2009, Obama delineated those principles, saying that any health reform measure should do the following:

1. Protect families' financial health (slowing the growth of out-of-pocket expenses and protecting people from bankruptcy due to catastrophic illness)
2. Make health insurance coverage more affordable (reducing administrative costs, wiping out unnecessary tests and services, limiting insurers' ability to charge higher premiums for certain populations)
3. Aim for insurance coverage universality
4. Provide portability of insurance coverage
5. Guarantee choice of health plans and providers (including keeping current ones)
6. Invest in disease prevention and wellness initiatives
7. Improve patient safety and healthcare quality
8. Maintain long-term fiscal sustainability (reducing cost growth, improving productivity, adding new revenue sources)

The extent to which these principles were brought to life in what eventually became the ACA lives along a spectrum. For example, health insurance was absolutely made more affordable for millions of people; disease prevention and wellness initiatives seem to be gaining momentum, though slowly; and universal insurance coverage was absolutely not achieved. Whatever the case with any particular principle, it is instructive to look to four key reforms that became law under the ACA as having paved the way for President Obama's overall vision to come to fruition. These four reforms essentially reordered long-standing relationships among health system stakeholders, including individuals, providers, insurers, employers, and governments. As a result of this reordering, all of these stakeholders were legally obligated to alter normative behaviors.

The first major change, known as the individual mandate, is a requirement that individuals maintain "minimum essential health coverage" (i.e., health insurance) or face financial penalties that are spelled out in the ACA. This requirement was a critically important beam in the ACA architecture because it created a new, large pool of individuals who pay premiums to insurance companies, and it created leverage for policymakers who were eager for the private insurers to accept many of the ACA's other insurance reforms that may otherwise have been unpalatable. For certain individuals whose socioeconomic status makes it impossible for them to purchase (or gain through an employer) the type of minimum coverage mandated by the ACA, and who do not qualify for Medicaid (even under the ACA expansion), federal subsidies are made available under the law. As discussed in more detail below, in 2017 Congress repealed the penalties associated with the individual mandate as part of the Tax Cut and Jobs Act.

The second fundamental change results from reforms that prohibit or curtail existing health insurer and health plan practices (these are the types of reforms, noted in the preceding paragraph, that all insurers—not just those who sell products through the new exchanges, described in the following paragraph—were forced to accept to reciprocate for the new group of premium payers they would insure as a result of the individual mandate). For example, the ACA prohibits insurers from considering an applicant's preexisting conditions when determining whether to insure the applicant, guarantees the renewability of an individual's existing insurance plan, requires insurers to cover certain preventive and immunization services, and guarantees coverage for dependent children who are 26 years old or younger.

The third key change is the creation of health insurance "exchanges" or "marketplaces" in each state. These are essentially online shopping sites, the purpose of which is to make it easier for individuals and small employers to compare and purchase health insurance. Because the ACA requires everyone to carry health insurance, and because the insurance marketplace has not historically been easy to navigate, policymakers forced the creation of regulated state-based exchanges to help with the purchase of individual and small-group insurance plans.

The final major reform is an expansion of the existing Medicaid program. This reform has the potential to dramatically increase the number of individuals who can gain access to insurance coverage—and thus access to better and more appropriate health care. Because states cannot be forced to implement this expansion (more on this to follow in the discussion of the U.S. Supreme Court's decision around the constitutionality of the ACA), and many states have thus far declined to implement the expansion, this potential has yet to become a reality. Although the ACA does not completely alter the way health insurance is provided by, say, establishing a single-payer system or even a large government-run insurance plan to compete with private insurers, the law makes significant philosophical and practical changes in how health insurance is regulated, structured, and administered. Indeed, as a result of the reforms and reordering just described, the ACA has resulted in 19 million people gaining insurance between 2010 and 2017, dropping the uninsured rate from 16% in 2010 to 11.1% in early 2017 (Blumberg, Holahan, Karpman, & Elmendorf, 2018). In addition, as a result of the essential health benefits requirement, there is a large segment of the population that is no longer underinsured because of insurance plans that do not offer comprehensive benefits.

Even so, many people contend that the ACA falls short in its reform of the healthcare delivery system. And in many cases they are correct. The ACA is most notable for the transformations it makes to health insurance—both access to it and its content—rather than for structural reforms made to the delivery system. Many provisions that focus on improving the healthcare delivery system, increasing the quality of care received by patients, reducing healthcare costs, and incentivizing providers to reconsider traditional methods of delivering care, often exist in the form of temporary pilot programs that may never be enacted permanently even if they prove to be valuable. Other analysts contend that these provisions were written as strongly as they could be at the time, given the political environment and data available to policymakers. According to this view, the ACA provides the secretary of the HHS with unprecedented authority to make the pilot programs permanent, and it would have been irresponsible to implement more permanent, wholesale changes without more evidence. In any case, as sweeping as the ACA is, it is far from being the last step that needs to be taken to improve how health care is provided in the United States.

President Trump's proclamations about the ACA have vacillated from supporting efforts to repeal and then replace the law, to repeal and replace it simultaneously, to let the ACA "implode" to force the Democrats to negotiate, to keep the existing law but make improvements to it (Graham, 2017). His administration's actions, however, have consistently undermined the ACA, making it more likely that the uninsured rate will increase, premiums will rise, and consumer protections will diminish. Examples of these actions are highlighted in **BOX 2**. In general, the administration's strategy appears to focus on (1) providing states with flexibility to interpret ACA requirements and (2) weakening the marketplaces by deterring insurers from participating in the exchanges and increasing prices for consumers purchasing products through the exchanges (Tworney, Berger, & Brady, 2018).

BOX 2 Select Trump Administration Executive Actions Relating to the ACA

- Issued Executive Order ordering federal agencies to begin dismantling the ACA "to the maximum extent permitted by law" and to grant exemptions or delay implementation of ACA provisions that impose a tax, fee, or other costs (January 2017)
- Issued an insurance regulation that made it more difficult for individuals to sign up for insurance during a special enrollment period, shortened the length of the enrollment period, lowered premium tax credits, made it easier for insurers to collect back premiums, and provided states more flexibility to define Essential Health Benefits (April 2017)
- Ended contracts to navigators that provided one-on-one enrollment assistance to consumers, slashed funding for enrollment outreach efforts, and limited weekend access to online enrollment functions (July–August 2017)
- Created an expanded option for employers who choose not to provide contraceptive coverage due to religious or moral reasons (October 2017)
- Ceased cost-sharing reduction payments to insurers (October 2017)
- Signed the Tax Cut and Jobs Act, which eliminated individual mandate penalties (December 2017)
- Proposed Association Health Plan (AHP) rules that would allow these plans to offer insurance products that are exempt from many ACA provisions, such as the Essential Health Benefits provision and another one that limits the charging of higher premiums based on one's age, gender, or occupation (January 2018)
- Issued guidance allowing work requirements to be applied to Medicaid recipients. Approved Kentucky's Medicaid waiver that includes work requirements, higher premiums, and coverage lockouts (January 2018) (Note that this waiver was subsequently vacated by a federal court and the question of whether states can mandate work requirements for Medicaid recipients is the subject of ongoing litigation.)
- Proposed rules to extend short-term limited duration health plans (that do not need to meet many of the ACA's requirements) from 3 months to 1 year (February 2018)
- Filed a brief in *Texas v. United States* declining to defend the constitutionality of the ACA (June 2018)
- Delayed risk-adjustment transfers that provide payments from insurers with low-risk pools to insurers with high-risk pools (July 2018)
- Slashed the budget (again) for enrollment outreach and navigation efforts (July 2018)

Source: Center on Budget and Policy Priorities, 2018.

We turn now to a more detailed discussion of the ACA's key components, including a review of how the administration's efforts have altered the law even though Congress has been unsuccessful in its efforts to repeal and replace the ACA.

Individual Mandate

An individual mandate is a requirement that individuals purchase health insurance. This is not a new idea. President Clinton proposed an individual mandate in 1993 as part of his Health Security Act, and other competing proposals at the time, including those supported by Republicans, also included an individual mandate. Massachusetts, the only state in the country to require that everyone older than 18 years have health insurance, included an individual mandate as one way to achieve that goal. A number of other countries, including the Netherlands, Switzerland, Germany, Japan, and Australia, have some form of an insurance mandate in their healthcare systems (Eibner & Nowak, 2018). During the 2008 election, Obama originally supported a mandate for children to be covered but suggested waiting to see if a mandate was necessary for adults after implementing other major health reform changes.

While the individual mandate is not a new idea and has been championed by both Republicans and Democrats at different times in history, it has proven to be a politically perilous route to reducing the number of uninsured. Opposition to the individual mandate has softened over time, but public opinion remains split and partisan. A 2017 poll taken during the debate about the Republican ACA repeal and replacement efforts found that 50% of respondents supported retaining the individual mandate, while 48% preferred to eliminate this provision (Agiesta, 2017). This represents a shift in favor of the mandate over a 2013 poll that found 58% of respondents opposed (Burke, 2013). Over half of Republicans (55%) opposed the individual mandate in 2017 as compared to 84% in 2013. Democrats remained supportive of the individual mandated, with 60% preferring to keep the mandate in place in 2017, similar to the 57% who felt that way in 2013 (Agiesta, 2017).

It appears that some individuals do not prefer to be told they have to purchase health insurance by the government, even if it is a choice they made on their own prior to the passage of the ACA. But issues such as affordability or difficulty using the federal exchange website were more likely to be cited as reasons for not having health insurance than political opposition to the mandate. A poll conducted shortly after the first enrollment period closed found that most people who remained uninsured cited affordability (39%) or job-related reasons (22%), while only 9% felt they did not want or need health insurance (Hamel, Firth, & Brodie, 2014). Understandably, affordability remains a top issue for the public. In a recent poll, all respondents (regardless of political leanings) ranked limiting the amount individuals pay for health care as their top priority (DiJulio, Kirzinger, Wu, & Brodie, 2017). Almost half (49%) were very worried or somewhat worried about not being able to afford healthcare services in the future (DiJulio et al., 2017).

Individual mandates can be set up in a variety of ways, but usually individuals who do not comply will be required to pay some sort of penalty. The penalty is intended to provide both an incentive to comply with the law and to raise funds to cover the cost of health care for those individuals who choose not to carry health insurance. Individual mandates are considered to be a cornerstone of health reform efforts because they ensure that everyone covered by the mandate will be in an insurance pool to help cover costs and share risk.

Starting in 2014, the ACA's individual mandate required that almost everyone purchase health insurance or pay a penalty. This penalty is phased in over time, beginning at the greater of $95 or 1% of taxable income per person in 2014 and growing to the greater of $695 or 2.5% of taxable income per person in 2016 and 2017. In subsequent years, the penalty amount increases through cost of living adjustments. The maximum penalty is the cost of the national average bronze plan sold through the marketplace.

The mandate is considered essential because without it people who are in poor health or otherwise expect to use more healthcare services will be more likely to purchase health insurance, whereas healthier people will be more likely to opt out of insurance coverage. This situation would lead to an insurance pool that is relatively sick and thus more expensive, a problem referred to as *adverse selection*. Adverse selection leads to a so-called "death spiral" as the insurance pool gets continually sicker and more expensive, encouraging more healthy people to opt out of coverage.

While there remains for now uncertainty about the exact impact of the recent decision to remove the penalties associated with the individual mandate, it is generally agreed that the uninsured rate and premiums will increase due to adverse selection. For example, the Congressional Budget Office estimates that eliminating the penalty associated with the mandate will reduce the number of people with insurance by 3 to 6 million and will increase individual market premiums by 10% between 2019 and 2021 (Eibner & Nowak, 2018). The Rand Compare microsimulation model found that by 2020 there would be 2.8 to 13 million fewer insured individuals and a premium change of a 1% decrease to a 13% increase, depending on the plan type and modeling assumptions (Eibner & Nowak, 2018).

Some policy experts consider the ACA's mandate to be too weak to be effective in any event, thus reducing, in their view, the impact of eliminating the penalties. In 2016, 6.5 million people paid an average fine of $70 for lack of coverage (Scott, 2018). Under the ACA, the penalties may not have been significant enough, nor the premium subsidies generous enough, to compel people to buy insurance. In addition, the United States does not enforce the mandate as vigorously as other countries do (Scott, 2018).

Due to fears of adverse selection, analysts have been closely watching how many young adults (ages 18–34 years), who are more likely to be healthy, sign up for health insurance. While ideally 40% of enrollees would be in this age range in order to prevent adverse selection, only about 28% of the 8 million enrollees signed up at the end of the first enrollment period in April 2014 were young adults (Galewitz, n.d.). About 45% of taxpayers who either paid a penalty for not having insurance or claimed an exemption from the mandate that year were younger than 35 years (Mills, 2016). While young adults have experienced a dramatic reduction in their uninsured rate, they still accounted for 37.9% of the uninsured in 2017 (Blumberg et al., 2018).

The individual mandate is also an essential feature of health reform because healthy individuals who choose not to purchase health insurance but then later need health care will likely receive some care even though they are uninsured. This is especially true if the individuals have the resources to pay for healthcare services. These individuals are referred to as *free riders* because they avoid paying premiums for health insurance during their healthy years but then enjoy the benefits of healthcare services when they become sick. In 2015, over 7 million people who earned more than $75,000 were uninsured (Census, 2015). Because it is likely that many of these individuals could have afforded to purchase health insurance, some analysts consider this evidence of the free-rider problem.

Politically, the individual mandate was essential to passing the ACA because it was the carrot that enticed health insurers to support health reform. The ACA includes a prohibition against excluding individuals who have preexisting conditions as a way to make health insurance available for those with health needs. Health insurers would have balked at being forced to enroll sicker individuals without a mandate intended to draw in healthier consumers as well. In addition, the mandate guaranteed new premium dollars from the new enrollees.

There are a number of exceptions to the individual mandate requirement. Individuals are exempt from purchasing insurance if their income is below the tax-filing threshold (in 2017 this was $10,400 for single people younger than 65 years and $20,800 for couples younger than 65 years), the lowest-cost plan option exceeds 8% of their income, they qualify for a religious exemption, they are incarcerated, they are undocumented immigrants, they were without coverage for less than 3 months, they are Native Americans, or they qualify as having a hardship. Based on a June 2013 HHS rule, hardship exemptions must be granted for individuals who experience an event that resulted in an unexpected increase in expenses such that purchasing health insurance would make it impossible to pay for necessities, such as food and shelter. The rule cites circumstances that would be considered under this exemption: homelessness, eviction, domestic violence, death of a close family member, bankruptcy, substantial recent medical debt, and disasters that substantially changed the individual's property (Exchange Establishment Standards, 2013). Hardship exemptions are also allowed for individuals who would have qualified for Medicaid had their state chosen to expand the program under the ACA, and other exemptions exist based on projected low income (Jost, 2013). In 2018, the Trump administration created four new exemption categories (Center for Consumer Information, 2018; HHS Notice of Benefit and Payment Parameters [HHS Benefit and Payment Rule], 2018). Individuals may apply for a hardship exemption if they (1) live in counties without marketplace plans, (2) live in counties with a single insurer, (3) object to abortion coverage, or (4) meet additional hardship circumstances, such as needing specialty care out-of-network (Keith, 2018b). Some have criticized the exemptions for being so broad as to swallow the individual mandate.

To some, the individual mandate remains controversial. In addition to believing that it represents unwarranted government intrusion into private decision making, opponents of the individual mandate argued after the ACA was passed that Congress did not have the legal authority to impose such a requirement. This argument is grounded in jurisprudence relating to the federal Constitution's Commerce Clause, which gives Congress the power to "regulate commerce with foreign nations, and among the several states, and with the Indian tribes" (U.S. Const. art. I, §8). Since the 1940s, the Supreme Court has interpreted the Commerce Clause to permit Congress to regulate economic activity that carries across state lines or local concerns that substantially affect interstate commerce, and several Commerce Clause cases have allowed the regulation of individual conduct (for example, the Supreme Court has upheld laws that prohibit an individual from refusing to interact with a minority and laws that regulate an individual's ability to grow wheat or marijuana for home consumption [*Heart of Atlanta Motel v. United States*, 1964]), and the regulation of

---

BOX 3 Discussion Questions

Are there alternatives to the individual mandate that accomplish the same goals without engendering so much political turmoil? Could policymakers have designed an incentive system that would be as effective as a mandate? What are the pros and cons of using a mandate versus an incentive? Can you think of incentives to encourage enrollment that have occurred in other parts of the healthcare system?

---

health insurance has also been deemed within the scope of the Commerce Clause (*Gonzales v. Raich*, 2005; *Wickard v. Filburn*, 1942).

Notwithstanding these cases, those who argued against the individual mandate contended that the Commerce Clause does not permit Congress to require an individual to purchase a service or good such as health insurance. In other words, the argument goes, an individual's decision not to purchase health insurance cannot be considered "economic activity" that Congress may regulate. Instead, it is argued, Congress is trying to regulate economic *in*activity—the decision not to purchase health insurance—and that this is not permitted under the Commerce Clause (Shapiro, 2010).

On the other hand, those who contend the Commerce Clause permits Congress to establish an individual mandate to purchase health insurance argue that everyone uses healthcare services at some point in their lives. Decisions regarding health insurance are an economic activity because no one can opt out of the healthcare market; that is, the decision individuals make is not whether to participate but how to participate in it. People will participate by purchasing health insurance now to cover the cost of future services or by paying out-of-pocket later at the time services are needed.

In the end, the Supreme Court upheld the individual mandate as a valid exercise of congressional *taxing* power; the court did, however, agree with those who maintained that the mandate was not permitted under the Commerce Clause. This outcome is described more fully later, when we provide an overview of the Supreme Court's June 2012 ruling on the constitutionality of the ACA.

State Health Insurance Exchanges/Marketplaces

The ACA established a new series of entities called health insurance exchanges (also referred to as marketplaces in federal documents) that are intended to create a more organized and competitive market for purchasing health insurance. These exchanges are state-based and geared toward those who purchase health insurance as individuals (through American Health Benefit Exchanges) or through small businesses (through the Small Business Health Options Program, or SHOP).

The SHOP exchange struggled from the start with implementation delays and much lower than anticipated enrollment (Aron-Dine, 2017). The Trump administration announced a rule that will effectively end the federally facilitated SHOP exchange as of January 2018 (HHS Notice of Benefit and Payment, 2018; Jost, 2017; Luhby, 2017b). The small employer tax credit will remain in place, but businesses will purchase SHOP-qualified plans directly from insurers instead of on the exchange. According to the new rule, Centers for Medicare and Medicaid Services (CMS) will be working to find more efficient and effective ways to increase insurance coverage for small business employees.

Starting in 2014, the exchanges for individuals began offering a variety of health insurance plans that meet ACA criteria regarding plan benefits, payments, and consumer information. The Congressional Budget Office (CBO) projects that by 2028, 8 million individuals will purchase their own health insurance through an exchange (CBO, 2018). This is significantly lower than earlier CBO estimates. Much of the difference is because fewer individuals are now projected to purchase unsubsidized plans on the exchange instead of directly from insurers in the nongroup market (Centers for Medicare and Medicaid Services, 2017). Because fewer employers than anticipated dropped their employee coverage, CBO overestimated the number of individuals who would shift from employer coverage to marketplace plans (CBO, 2017c; Jost, 2016). In addition, CBO expects 5 million fewer individuals to purchase nongroup coverage, including marketplace coverage, as a result of the individual mandate penalty repeal (CBO, 2017d).

The exchanges are a critical component of health reform because it would be untenable to require individuals to purchase health insurance without also making comprehensive and affordable health insurance options available. Individuals often face expensive and less comprehensive health insurance choices because their insurance pools are not extensive enough that the premiums paid by healthy individuals offset the costs associated with sicker individuals. The exchanges are intended to create a new market by bringing together large numbers of individuals to create wider insurance pools. Individuals are eligible to purchase health insurance through an exchange if they live in the state where the exchange operates, are U.S. citizens or legal immigrants, and are not incarcerated. Additional requirements must be met, however, to obtain subsidies that reduce the cost of health insurance. Subsidies are available to individuals who meet the previously mentioned requirements and who also do not have access to affordable (as defined by the ACA) employer-sponsored insurance, meet specified income requirements, file taxes jointly (if married), and are not eligible for Medicaid, Medicare, or the Children's Health Insurance Program (CHIP) (KFF, n.d.b).

Under the ACA, states have three main options when it came to exchanges: they can build their own, enter into a partnership with the federal government, or ignore the process altogether and thus default into what is referred to as a federally facilitated marketplace (FFM; this federally facilitated exchange was mandated by the ACA for states that were not willing or able to establish a state exchange or a partnership exchange). In a state-run exchange, the state either handles all functions or may use the federal information technology (IT) platform; in a partnership exchange, states may administer plan management functions, in-person consumer assistance functions, or both, with HHS performing remaining responsibilities; and in the FFM, HHS performs all functions. Whatever the structure, the exchanges for individuals were required to be up and running by January 1, 2014. At the time of this writing, the breakdown is as follows: 17 states and the District of Colombia built their own exchange (with 5 of the states using the federal IT platform); 6 set up partnership exchanges; and 28 states defaulted to the FFM (KFF, 2018). States also may form a regional exchange with other states or allow multiple exchanges within one state as long as each exchange covers a distinct geographic area. In addition, the federal Office of Personnel Management is required to offer at least two multistate plans within each exchange to provide individuals and businesses with additional choices.

The ACA requires the exchanges to ensure that plans meet other requirements of participating in the exchange. These requirements relate to marketing practices, provider networks, outreach and enrollment, insurance market regulations, and the provision of information in plain language. In addition, the entity running the exchange must provide a call center for customers, maintain a website, develop uniform applications, provide information regarding eligibility for public programs, assist individuals in calculating their tax credits, and certify individuals who are exempt from the individual mandate requirement.

As noted earlier, the Trump administration actions undermining the ACA have focused on strategies that weaken the ACA marketplaces. One way to accomplish this goal is to allow cheaper alternatives for individuals to purchase health insurance in the nongroup market outside of the exchanges. In general, a cheaper alternative is likely to have less comprehensive benefits and/or higher cost-sharing for the individual. The administration's rule expanding both Association Health Plans (AHPs) and short-term limited-duration plans are part of this strategy. AHPs allow business associations and other organizations to join together to provide fringe benefits, including health insurance (CBO, 2018). Short-term plans were designed to fill in

---

BOX 4   Provider Networks

An emerging policy and care delivery issue has been the question of whether provider networks available in plans offered in the exchanges are adequate. Prior to the ACA, insurers could control costs through a variety of mechanisms, including limiting benefits, excluding consumers with preexisting conditions, and using medical underwriting to charge higher premiums to higher-risk individuals and groups. Plans would compete with each other based on price, benefits, cost-sharing, and other features. The ACA includes a variety of rules that eliminate these options, such as prohibition of exclusions based on preexisting conditions, guaranteed issue requirements, community rating requirements, essential health benefit requirements, and actuarial tiering of plans. As a result of ACA restrictions, many plans are trying to control costs by limiting provider networks and/or provider reimbursement. Of course, some providers may choose not to participate in exchange plans if the reimbursement is not sufficient.

Many consumers who purchase plans in an exchange choose plans based on the premium price and indicate they would prefer cheaper plans with narrow networks as opposed to expensive plans with broader networks. On the other hand, consumers who purchase plans through employer-sponsored insurance often prefer broader networks, even if the coverage is more expensive. Complaints about narrow networks range from consumers being disappointed that their usual doctor or local hospital is not in network, to questions about access to care, network transparency, and quality of care. Several lawsuits have been filed against plans regarding network transparency and provider terminations. In 2014 the Office of the Insurance Commissioner issued federal rules regarding network adequacy in individual and small-group plans, and CMS continues to issue guidance regarding network adequacy for qualified health plans. State responses to network adequacy concerns have spanned the gamut, from Massachusetts requiring plans to develop tiered and narrow networks to promote cost savings, to several failed attempts by state legislatures to pass "any willing provider" laws that require insurers to include any provider willing to accept the insurers' terms.

Data From: McDermott Will & Emery. Challenges facing "narrow" provider networks on the ACA health insurance exchanges. http://www.mwe.com/files/Uploads/Documents/News/Challenges-Facing-Narrow-Provider-Networks.pdf. Published April 20, 2015. Accessed July 7, 2015.

a temporary insurance coverage gap and are not renewable (Pollitz, Long, Semanskee, & Kamal, 2018).

Both types of plans are likely to "limit benefits, be priced on the basis of an individuals health status, and impose lifetime and annual spending limits, and insurers could reject applicants on the basis of their health and any preexisting condition" (CBO, 2018, p. 10). One review of short-term plans found that 71% did not cover outpatient prescription drugs, 62% did not cover substance abuse services, 43% did not cover mental health services, and no plans covered maternity care (Pollitz et al., 2018). By allowing insurers to offer nongroup plans that do not have to comply with these ACA provisions, it is possible to create cheaper and skimpier insurance products. As a result, adverse selection is likely to occur in the exchange plans as healthier individuals who do not believe they need a comprehensive plan—or do not want to pay a higher premium to participate in one—will leave the exchange plan and move to a cheaper nongroup option. CBO estimates that 6 million people will enroll in AHPs or short-term plans by 2023 (CBO, 2018).

Another way to weaken ACA marketplaces is to make it more difficult to enroll in marketplace plans. Several Trump administration policies create barriers to enrollment. These policies include shortening the enrollment period, limiting advertising and other outreach during the enrollment period, reducing the budget for "navigators" who assist consumers in understanding and enrolling in marketplace plans, and limiting weekend online enrollment functions through the official HealthCare.gov website (Center for American Progress, 2018).

Essential Health Benefit Requirement

All qualified health plans that participate in an exchange (as well as individual and small-group plans outside of the exchanges) must offer a standard benefit package called essential health benefits (EHBs) (**BOX 5**) (Giovannelli, Lucia, & Corlette, 2014). This requirement represents the first time private health insurance plans have been subject to a federal standard regarding what benefits must be offered.

BOX 5 Essential Health Benefits

All plans in the state exchanges must offer the following benefits:

- Ambulatory patient services
- Emergency services
- Hospitalization
- Maternity and newborn care
- Mental health services and substance use disorder services, including behavioral health treatment
- Prescription drugs
- Rehabilitative and habilitative services and devices (rehabilitative therapies improve, maintain, or prevent deterioration of functions that have been acquired [e.g., after an adult has surgery], whereas habilitative therapies are provided to achieve functions and skills never acquired [e.g., as with a developmentally disabled child])
- Laboratory services
- Prevention and wellness services and chronic disease management services
- Pediatric services, including vision and dental services

The ACA requires the secretary of HHS to ensure the scope of benefits is equal to the benefit level found in a "typical employer plan." Plans may not design their benefit or reimbursement packages in ways that discriminate based on age, disability, or expected length of life (Rosenbaum, Teitelbaum, & Hayes, 2011).

While the ACA outlines 10 categories of services that must be provided in the EHB package, the federal regulatory process left states with significant discretion about how they implemented this requirement. States have a choice of 10 federally approved health plans to serve as a benchmark to determine the breadth of the services covered under the EHB categories. These approved benchmark plans include the largest three small-group plans available in the state, the largest three state-employee health plans in the state, the largest three Federal Employee Health Benefit Program plan options for federal employees, or the state's largest commercial HMO (Giovannelli et al., 2014). In 2017, 26 states did not choose a benchmark plan and were defaulted to the largest small-group plan offered in that state (Keith, 2017). Whether by choice or default, most states are using small-group plans, which are often less generous than large-group plans, as their benefit benchmark (Giovannelli, Volk, Lucia, William, & Connor, 2015). The Trump administration added another benchmarking option through its definition of a "typical employer plan," effective in 2020. In addition to the 10 benchmark plans discussed, states may also use any of the five largest (by enrollment) group health insurance products in the state that meet certain requirements (Keith, 2018b). The administration further expanded state choice in 2020 by allowing states to select annually whether to (1) use another state's entire 2017 benchmark plan, (2) replace one or more of its EHB categories with another state's EHB categories, or (3) choose a new EHB benchmark plan (Keith, 2018b).

Benchmark plans are subject to minimum and maximum standards. At a minimum, the benchmark plans must meet the "typical employer plan" standard. At a maximum, also known as the generosity test, the benchmark plan cannot be more generous than the most generous comparison plan (Keith, 2018b). The comparison plans are the state's 2017 benchmark and the state's three or four largest (by enrollment) small-group health plans (Keith, 2018b). The federal government will defer to the state's interpretation of plan benefits and limits (Keith, 2018b).

The Trump administration has also changed the rules regarding substituting benefits. Under the Obama administration, insurers were allowed to substitute benefits *within* an EHB category, but not *across* EHB categories, as long as the substitution was actuarially equivalent to the benefit it was replacing. Under the Trump administration, states may substitute actuarially equivalent benefits both *within* and *across* EHB categories (Keith, 2018b). An example of a *within* EHB substitution could be replacing a blood screen (lab test) for ovarian cancer with coverage of a blood screen for high cholesterol, a different, but actuarially equivalent, laboratory test (Giovannelli et al., 2014). An *across* EHB substitution would be replacing one type of service (e.g., an inpatient hospital service) with a completely different type of service (e.g., an outpatient physician service). Substitution is not permitted for prescription drugs.

Critics of the *across* substitution rule are concerned that plans will substitute out select benefits so that they do not appeal to certain high-risk individuals. In addition, once a service is not considered an EHB, it is no longer subject to ACA protections, such as lifetime or annual dollar limits, nor is it used to calculate premium subsidies and cost-sharing reductions (Keith, 2018b). Nine states and the

District of Columbia prohibited *within* category substitution in 2014 (Giovannelli et al., 2014). As with many of the Trump administration changes, states will have the final say over whether and how they choose to take advantage of this flexibility.

Further variation across the states may occur with habilitative service coverage and state benefit mandates. Habilitative services assist individuals with gaining or maintaining functional skills (e.g., speaking, walking). Prior to ACA passage, coverage for and the definition of habilitative services varied significantly. As part of ACA implementation, federal regulators permitted states to use the habilitative services definition in their benchmark plan (if there was such coverage), create their own coverage definition, or let the insurers define the coverage benefit (Giovannelli et al., 2014). As a result, the definition of habilitative services may differ across states and within states. Finally, some states passed laws that required insurers in their states to cover a particular benefit, such as obesity management services. Any benefit mandates that were in place before 2012 were incorporated into that state's EHB package, meaning the variation that was in place prior to health reform is likely to continue. It is less likely that states will add new benefit mandates at this time because if a state plans to include any services beyond the essential health benefits package that were not mandated prior to 2012, the state must defray the cost of the additional service through a payment to the enrollee or the plan. In addition, the new generosity test means that it may be more difficult for states to choose a benchmark that includes an expensive mandate (Keith, 2018b).

In the lead-up to passage of the ACA, there was significant debate about whether to allow or require plans to offer abortion and contraceptive services. In fact, the abortion debate was so divisive it almost doomed the entire health reform bill at the 11th hour. A compromise was reached with the intent of keeping the status quo regarding federal funding for abortion services (i.e., limit federal funding for abortion services to cases where the life of the pregnant woman is in danger or the pregnancy is a result of rape or incest). Under the compromise, states may enact a law that prohibits plans that participate in their state exchanges from providing abortion services.

The ACA also provides coverage, without any cost-sharing, for all contraception methods approved by the Food and Drug Administration. While contraception is considered a preventive service under the EHB standard, it is not specifically listed in the statute (nor are other preventive services; instead the statute references guidelines such as the U.S. Preventive Services Task Force A and B recommendations). Contraceptive coverage is part of a separate provision that includes women's preventive services identified by the Health Resources and Services Administration. Because this guideline is created by an administrative agency, each successive administration has the power to change the list of approved women's preventive services without needing congressional approval. The Obama administration exempted certain entities from being required to provide contraception coverage due to religious objections (Coverage Preventive Services, 2013). The required breadth of this exemption is the subject of numerous lawsuits and remains unsettled at this time. The Trump administration is considering a new administrative rule that would significantly broaden the group of employers and insurers who would qualify for the exemption based on religious or moral grounds (Pear, 2017).

Given the Trump administration's policies intended to restrict access to abortion services (e.g., supporting the defunding of Planned Parenthood) and contraceptive devices (e.g., by broadening the religious objection exemption), it is worth noting what actions states have taken on these issues. As of June 2018, 11 states have enacted laws that restrict abortion coverage in all private plans in the state, 25 states restrict abortion coverage in private plans offered through their exchange, and 21 states restrict abortion coverage in public employee plans (Guttmacher Institute, n.d.; Guttmacher Institute, 2018a). If a state does not enact such a law and a plan chooses to offer abortion services in other circumstances, the plan must create separate financial accounts to ensure that federal premium and cost-sharing subsidies are not used toward those abortion services. In addition, at least one of the multistate plans is required not to provide abortion services beyond those that are currently allowed with federal funding. As with most compromises, neither side was entirely pleased with the outcome. Those who want more restrictive abortion policies found the separate accounting process to be a meaningless exercise, whereas those who want more permissive abortion policies were disturbed by the ability of states to prohibit plans from offering abortion services. As of June 2018, 29 states require insurance plans to cover the full range of contraceptive drugs, 9 states prohibit cost-sharing for contraceptives, and 5 states prohibit other restrictions and delays by insurers. At the same time, 21 states exempt select employers and insurers from providing contraceptive coverage based on religious objections (Guttmacher Institute, 2018b).

The ACA also created a "catastrophic coverage" option that must include EHBs (KFF, n.d.). A catastrophic plan may be offered only to individuals younger than 30 years who would be exempt from the individual mandate requirement due to hardship or affordability exemptions. These plans require coverage of EHBs, certain preventive services without cost-sharing, and at least three primary care visits each year before meeting the deductible (KFF, n.d.). Individuals may not use premium tax credits to subsidize catastrophic plans, which typically have low premiums but very high deductibles.

Premium and Cost-Sharing Subsidies

One key difference among the exchange plans is the cost to the enrollee. Four levels of plans may be offered, and they are distinguished by their actuarial value. Actuarial value is the average share of covered benefits generally paid by the insurer based on the cost-sharing provisions in the plan. The higher the actuarial value, the more the plan pays for a given set of services. For example, in a plan with 70% actuarial value,

BOX 6 Discussion Questions

There was a lengthy debate about whether to include a public option in health reform. A public option is some type of government-run health plan that would be available to compete with private plans. A public option could exist within the health exchange model or outside of it. Instead of a public option, Congress voted to require the Office of Personnel Management, which runs the Federal Employees Health Benefit Program, to contract with at least two multistate plans in every state health insurance exchange.

What are the pros and cons of having a public option? Does the Office of Personnel Management compromise achieve all or some of the goals of having a public option? Why do you believe the Office of Personnel Management compromise was acceptable to legislators but the public option was not?

the plan pays 70% of the cost of services on average across all enrollees, while enrollees pay 30%. Actuarial value is set by average cost, but any single enrollee in that plan may pay more or less than 30% of the cost of services. In general, plans with a higher actuarial value will also have higher premiums to cover the cost of providing services to enrollees. A plan with lower premiums could have higher cost-sharing (co-pays or deductibles) to offset the lower premium. The four ACA-approved plan levels by actuarial value are bronze (60% actuarial value), silver (70% actuarial value), gold (80% actuarial value), and platinum (90% actuarial value). Plans must offer at least one silver-level and one gold-level option in each exchange in which they participate.

The ACA includes premium tax credits and cost-sharing subsidies (CSRs) to help make it affordable for people to purchase health insurance in a state exchange. Given the mandate to purchase insurance, it was necessary to include some assistance to make it possible for low-income individuals to comply with the new requirement. The tax credits and subsidies were available starting in 2014, the same year the individual mandate and the state health insurance exchanges went into effect. In 2017, 8.7 million people (84% of marketplace enrollees) received a premium tax credit, and 5.9 million people (57% of marketplace enrollees) received a CSR (KFF, 2017a).

Premium tax credits are available to individuals who are eligible to purchase health insurance in state exchanges; have incomes between 100% and 400% of the federal poverty level; are not eligible for Medicaid, CHIP, or Medicare; and do not have access to affordable employer-sponsored health insurance. (An employer plan is not considered affordable if it does not cover at least 60% of covered benefits or if the employee's share of premium contributions exceeds 9.5% of the employee's income.) In 2018, 400% of the poverty level was $48,560 for an individual and $100,400 for a family of four (Office of Assistant Secretary for Planning and Evaluation, 2018). The tax credits are advanceable and refundable, meaning they are available when health insurance is purchased and regardless of whether the individual owes any taxes. CSRs (i.e., federal funds provided to assist individuals with the purchase of insurance) are available to people who earn between 100% and 250% of the poverty level. Under the ACA, individuals with income less than 133% of the poverty level will be eligible for Medicaid beginning in 2014 in those states that elected to implement the ACA's Medicaid eligibility expansion.

The amount of the premium tax credit is tiered based on income and set so individuals will not have to pay more than a certain percentage of their income on premiums (**TABLE 1**). The tax credit amount is based on the cost of the second-lowest-cost silver plan in the exchange and location where the individual is eligible to purchase insurance. Individuals who want to purchase a more expensive plan have to pay the difference in cost between the second-lowest-cost silver plan and the plan they prefer to purchase. Under the ACA, HHS will adjust the premium people are expected to pay to reflect that premium costs typically grow faster than income levels.

For example, assume Bob's income is 250% of poverty (about $31,000 for an individual), and the cost of the second-lowest-cost silver plan in Bob's area is $5,700. Under the premium tax credit schedule, Bob will pay no more than 8.05% of his income, or $2,495. Bob's tax credit is $3,205, which is $5,700 minus $2,495 (KFF, n.d.).

CSRs are available to help low-income people reduce the amount of out-of-pocket spending on health insurance (**TABLE 2**). The subsidies are tiered by income level and set so that plans pay a higher percentage of service costs. In other words, they are set to increase the actuarial value of the plan for low-income individuals.

TABLE 1 Premium Tax Credit Schedule	
Income Level by Federal Poverty Level (FPL)	**Premium as a Percentage of Income**
100–133% FPL	2% of income
133–150% FPL	3–4% of income
150–200% FPL	4–6.3% of income
200–250% FPL	6.3–8.05% of income
250–300% FPL	8.05–9.5% of income
300–400% FPL	9.5% of income

TABLE 2 Cost-Sharing Subsidy Schedule	
Income Level by Federal Poverty Level (FPL)	**Actuarial Value**
100–150% FPL	94%
150–200% FPL	87%
200–250% FPL	73%

Under the ACA, insurers receive payments from the federal government to cover the expense of providing CSRs to their low-income enrollees. Nearly 6 million enrollees qualified for CSRs in 2017, which was expected to cost the federal government $7 billion (Liptak, Luhby, & Mattingly, 2017). These payments to insurers have been the subject of litigation brought by House Republicans, originally during the Obama administration (the case was first known as *House v. Burwell*, then it was retitled *House v. Price* to account for a new HHS Secretary, and currently the case has been retitled *House v. Azar* for the same reason). Initially, the federal trial court agreed with the plaintiffs' claim that the subsidies should not be funded because Congress did not appropriate money for that purpose. The Obama administration appealed, after which the case was put on hold during multiple delays. In October 2017, the Trump administration announced that it would no longer make CSR payments to insurers, and as a result the various parties to the lawsuit—House Republicans, the Trump administration, and several states (which had been granted a request along the way to intervene in the case)—started to negotiate a settlement.

Having reached a conditional settlement in December 2017, the parties asked the original trial judge to issue an "indicative ruling" that she would vacate her original order on CSR payments if the case were sent back to her from the appellate court (to which the Obama administration had appealed some years earlier) without a ruling on the merits. At the request of the parties, the appellate court did just that; it dismissed the appeal and sent the case back to the trial court. In turn, the trial judge vacated her initial decision. That said, the CSR saga is not over: several state attorneys general filed a lawsuit against HHS over its decision to end the CSR payments, and some insurers have done the same.

The ACA requires insurers to offer low-income enrollees reduced deductibles and co-payments. Without CSR payments to cover the costs of those reductions, insurers will increase premiums to make up for lost revenue and/or leave the insurance market altogether (Liptak et al., 2017). While the amount varies by state, it is estimated that cessation of CSR payments led to an average premium increase of 19% in 2018 (Kamal, Semanskee, Long, Claxton, & Leavitt, 2017). Many insurers are targeting their premium increase just to the silver plan, a strategy known as "silver loading" (Keith, 2018c). By doing so, they are maximizing premium tax credits they receive, which are tied to silver plan costs. In addition, since consumers may use their tax credits for any plan, many could enroll in a bronze or gold plan at a lower cost than in prior years. While the Trump administration could prohibit silver loading, they have not done so to date (Keith, 2018c). Ironically, it is estimated that the cost to the federal government for not making the CSR payments is $2 billion *more* than it would be if it simple made the payments, because of the higher premium tax credits owed (Fise, 2017).

In addition to the premium tax credits and CSRs, the ACA limits the overall amount of out-of-pocket costs paid by individuals with incomes up to 400% of poverty (**TABLE 3**). The limits are based on the maximum out-of-pocket costs for health

TABLE 3 Out-of-Pocket Spending Limits

Income Level by Federal Poverty Level (FPL)	Out-of-Pocket Limit
100–200% FPL	2/3 of maximum
200–300% FPL	1/2 of maximum
300–400% FPL	1/3 of maximum

BOX 7 Discussion Questions

CBO estimates that premium subsidies and CSRs will cost the federal government $760 billion over the years 2019–2028 (CBO, 2018). Is this a good use of resources? Are these subsidies well designed? Are they sufficient to make health insurance affordable? Do they cover people with incomes that are too high? Should they cover more people?

savings accounts ($6,650 for single coverage, $13,300 for family coverage in 2018) and will be indexed annually.

The insurance subsidies have been at the center of litigation and political maneuvering and are discussed later. These subsidies—and, in turn, the viability of the ACA overall—were at risk due to a lawsuit that challenged the legality of subsidies provided to the millions of people in the states that use a federally operated insurance exchange instead of setting up a state-based exchange (Taylor, Saenz, & Levine, 2015). Congress wrote in the ACA that federal subsidies were available to individuals who purchased health insurance through exchanges that were "established by the State." As part of the law's implementation process, the Internal Revenue Service (IRS) issued a regulation indicating that federal subsidies were available to individuals who purchased health insurance in either state-run or federally operated exchanges (Health Insurance Premium, 2012). The individuals who brought the lawsuit argued that the IRS regulation was unlawful because it contradicted the language of the ACA. In essence, the court case boiled down to the meaning of the four words "established by the State": when read contextually against the rest of the ACA, were federally operated exchanges included in exchanges "established by the State," or were federal subsidies reserved only for individuals in states that established their own state-run exchange?

In a 6–3 decision in *King v. Burwell*, the U.S. Supreme Court upheld the ACA's statutory and regulatory scheme, allowing federal subsidies to flow to individuals who purchase insurance in both state-run and federally operated exchanges. Instead of reading the four words in question in a vacuum, Chief Justice Roberts, writing for the majority, viewed the phrase "established by the State" in the context of the overall purpose of the law. Doing otherwise, according to the court, would bring about "the type of calamitous result [insurance market failure] that Congress plainly meant to avoid" in crafting the ACA in the first place. Noting that the court's duty is to construe statutes as a whole, not "isolated provisions," Chief Justice Roberts wrote the following:

> Congress passed the Affordable Care Act to improve health insurance markets, not to destroy them. If at all possible, we must interpret the [ACA] in a way that is consistent with the former, and avoids the latter. [The IRS regulation] can fairly be read consistent with what we see as Congress's plan, and that is the reading we adopt. (*King v. Burwell*, 2015)

In upholding the subsidies, the court differed in its reasoning from some lower federal courts that nonetheless also upheld the subsidies across all exchanges. These lower courts found the ACA's subsidy language ambiguous and therefore deferred to the agency (the IRS) that was tasked with interpreting the statute. In a critical move, the Supreme Court instead ruled that because the availability of tax credits was an issue with "deep economic and political significance" to the country, the meaning of the subsidy language should be interpreted by the court itself, rather than left to agency discretion. This decision means that the only way the subsidy language can be altered in the future is through congressional action, rather than by a future president whose administration might reinterpret the language more narrowly. Thus, it is far more likely that the subsidies will remain available in all exchanges—regardless of whether a state or the federal government operates them—going forward.

In addition to saving insurance subsidies for millions of Americans, the decision in *King v. Burwell* could have additional ramifications. Taken in conjunction with *NFIB v. Sebelius* (the 2012 Supreme Court decision upholding the constitutionality of the ACA), lower courts may read *King*'s direction to interpret the ACA as a congressional effort to improve insurance markets as a signal to forestall future litigation against the law. Furthermore, in states that have had difficulty setting up or operating their own exchange, the decision may encourage them to rely on the federal exchange apparatus; because there is no longer the threat that insurance subsidies could be easily untethered from federally facilitated exchanges, the use of such an exchange could become relatively more attractive.

Employer Mandate

As written in the ACA, employers with 50 or more employees and at least 1 employee who qualifies for a tax credit were required to offer affordable health insurance or pay a penalty beginning in 2014. The Obama administration twice delayed implementation of the mandate to smooth the transition, but the mandate itself did not change. Under the mandate, covered employers have three options: (1) provide affordable health insurance and not pay a penalty, (2) provide health insurance not considered affordable and pay a penalty, or (3) do not provide health insurance and pay a penalty. The penalties are based on whether an employer offers health insurance and whether any full-time employees take a premium tax credit. The amount of the penalty increases over time based on the national increase in premium costs. The employer mandate was put in place to encourage employers to continue offering or start offering health insurance. Without such a mandate, employers may have found it profitable not to offer health insurance and let their employees purchase health insurance through state exchanges, shifting more of the costs of health reform to the public sector and taxpayers.

For employers that do not offer health insurance and have at least one full-time employee who takes the premium tax credit, the penalty is $2,000 per employee after the first 30 employees. In other words, if such an employer has 50 employees, the employer would pay a $40,000 penalty ($2,000 × 20 employees).

Employers that offer health insurance do not pay a penalty if the insurance is considered affordable. Insurance is affordable if the plan has an actuarial value of at least 60% or if the premiums do not cost more than 9.5% of an employee's income. Employees who would have to pay more than 9.5% of their income on premiums have the option to purchase insurance through an exchange and receive a premium tax credit.

Employers who provide unaffordable insurance have to pay a penalty for each employee who takes a tax credit, not counting the first 30 employees (the 30-employee exception was included in the law due to Congress's concern about the impact of the employer mandate on small businesses). The penalty is $3,000 per employee who takes a tax credit but may not exceed $2,000 times the number of employees over 30. For example, if the employer has 50 employees and offers unaffordable coverage, the employer would pay a maximum penalty of $40,000 ($2,000 × 20). If only 10 employees take a tax credit, the penalty would be $30,000 ($3,000 × 10). If all 50 employees take a tax credit, the penalty would be $40,000, which is the maximum penalty allowed, not $150,000 ($3,000 × 50).

Given their smaller pool of employees, small businesses have often found it quite expensive to offer health insurance to their employees. In addition to exempting businesses with fewer than 50 employees from the employer mandate (and creating a health insurance exchange for small businesses), Congress also included a small business tax credit to encourage these employers to provide coverage. Employers are eligible for the tax credit if they have fewer than 25 full-time-equivalent employees, average annual wages under $50,000, and pay for at least half of the cost of health insurance coverage for their employees. The tax credit covers a portion of the cost of the employer's contribution toward employees' premiums. The credit is capped based on the average premium costs in the employer's geographic area and phases out as firm size and annual wages increase.

Because the employer mandate (and other provisions) will lead to increased costs for certain employers, some of these employers may be influenced to offset new costs by employing more part-time workers (at the expense of full-time employment) and/or capping the number of workers they hire at 49 to avoid the mandate (Blumberg, Holahan, & Buettgens, 2014). While several analyses indicate that the ACA's effects to the labor market may in fact be modest (Abraham & Royalty, 2017; Blumberg et al., 2014), the authors of one study (Blumberg et al., 2014) nonetheless go so far as to advocate for eliminating the employer mandate altogether. They argue that doing so would actually not reduce overall insurance coverage significantly, would eliminate any market distortions that could result from changes in employer hiring practices, and would have the added benefit of lessening employer opposition to the ACA (Blumberg et al., 2014).

Changes to the Private Insurance Market

In addition to creating a new marketplace for private insurance through state exchanges, the ACA includes a variety of changes to private health insurance rules and requirements. These requirements cover everything from rate setting, to benefits, to who must be covered. Although the overall health reform law is controversial, many of these private market reforms have overwhelming support. Together, these changes filled in gaps left by the private market that many people believed were unfair to consumers.

The following coverage changes took effect in 2010:

- **Preexisting conditions:** Individual and group plans may not exclude children due to their health status or based on preexisting conditions.
- **Dependent coverage:** Individual and group plans must provide dependent coverage up to age 26 years.
- **Preventive services:** New health plans may not impose cost-sharing for certain preventive services, including the following:
  - Preventive services with an A or B rating from the U.S. Preventive Services Task Force
  - Immunizations recommended by the Centers for Disease Control and Prevention's Advisory Committee on Immunization Practice
  - Preventive care and screening for women based on guidelines to be issued by the Health Resources and Services Administration
- **Coverage limits:** Individual and group plans may not impose lifetime dollar limits on coverage (and the ability to impose annual limits on the dollar value of coverage is prohibited as of 2014).
- **Rescission:** Individual and group plans may not rescind coverage except in the case of fraud.
- **Appeals:** New health insurance plans must have an effective appeals process that includes an external review option.

Congress also focused on the issue of how insurers determine premium rates and what they spend those resources on within their plans. The ACA charged HHS with establishing an annual process to review "unreasonable" increases in premiums (ACA, 2010, §1003). The 2019 benefit and payment rules change the definition of "unreasonable" from a 10% to a 15% increase and exempt student health services from the review requirements (Keith, 2018d). As of 2016, 43 states and the District of Columbia had some type of rate review law in place for all of their insurance markets, and the federal process is intended to work with, not preempt, those state laws (National Conference of State Legislators, 2016). These states must post all proposed increases at the same time and all final rate increases at the same time and must provide CMS with 5 days' notice of rate increases (Keith, 2018d).

In addition, the ACA requires that plans spend at least 85% (large-group plans) or 80% (small-group or individual plans) of their premium dollars on medical care and quality improvement services, not administrative or other expenses (e.g., profits). Regulations clarifying this medical loss ratio (MLR), as it is called, took effect on January 1, 2011 (Health Insurance Issuers, 2010). Insurers must provide enrollees with a rebate if they do not spend the requisite percentage on clinical and quality improvement services. Initially, insurers paid significant rebates to consumers ($1 billion in 2011), but by 2016 only 1.5% of enrollees received rebates as insurers improved their MLR to 92% in the individual market and 86% in the small-group market (Keith, 2018d). Under the 2019 benefit and payment rules, insurers may automatically claim 0.8% of earned premiums for quality improvement without supplying verifying documentation. This will raise the MLR rate for most insurers (Keith, 2018d). The rule also eases standards for seeking an MLR adjustment in the individual market. CMS projects that 22 states will seek such an adjustment, resulting in consumer rebate reductions of $52 to $64 million annually (Keith, 2018d).

A number of significant insurance changes took place in 2014 alongside implementation of the individual mandate and health insurance exchanges:

- **Guaranteed issue and renewability:** Individual and group plans may not exclude or charge more to individuals based on preexisting conditions or health status in the individual market, small-group market, and exchanges.
- **Rate variation limits:** Premium rates may vary based only on age, geographic area, family composition, and tobacco use in the individual market, small-group market, and exchanges.
- **Coverage limits:** Individual and group plans may not place annual dollar limits on coverage.
- **Essential health benefits:** Insurers providing coverage to small businesses or individuals and in the exchanges have to provide essential health benefits through one of four plan categories (bronze, silver, gold, or platinum) and adhere to annual cost-sharing limits.
- **Wellness plans:** Employers may offer rewards that reduce the cost of coverage to employees for participating in a wellness plan.

These private market changes do not affect all plans equally. Plans in small-group or nongroup markets must follow these rules whether or not they are offered in an exchange. However, the ACA included two significant exceptions to these reforms. First, insurance plans that were in existence when the ACA was signed into law are referred to as "grandfathered plans" and are subject to some, but not all, of the new rules. The grandfathered plans must follow new requirements relating to preexisting conditions, lifetime and annual limits, waiting period limits, and dependent coverage rules. These plans are exempt, however, from having to provide essential health benefits, preventive services without co-pays, and limited cost-sharing, although many of the large employer plans already have some of these features (Healthcare.gov, n.d.). A plan may retain its grandfathered status as long as it does not make significant changes to plan benefits or cost-sharing rules. If it loses its grandfathered status, the plan will have to meet all applicable requirements. In 2017, 23% of all employers offered at least one grandfathered plan, and 17% of covered workers were enrolled in a grandfathered plan (KFF and Health Research and Educational Trust [HRET], 2017, Section 13).

The second major exception is for self-funded plans. In these plans, an employer does not buy insurance from a company but instead takes on the insurance risk itself. Self-funded plans are exempt from state law and subject to federal rules under ERISA. Self-funded plans must adhere to ACA rules regarding dependent coverage, cost-sharing for preventive services, annual and lifetime limits, and waiting period limits, but do not need to comply with essential health benefit requirements (Commercial Insurance, 2012)

Financing Health Reform

Congress financed health reform primarily through Medicare and Medicaid savings, excise taxes and fees on the healthcare industry, changes to the income tax code, a tax on some health insurance plans, and expected individual and employer payments for violating insurance mandates. Several of these financing changes were made as part of the deals the Obama administration struck with various stakeholders.

The ACA's main financing features are as follows:

- **Medicare provider reimbursement:** Reduces "market basket" or cost updates for inpatient and outpatient hospital reimbursement and reduces payments for preventable hospital readmissions and hospital-acquired infections. This feature includes productivity adjustments (an adjustment in the Medicare physician fee schedule pertaining to physician productivity) for certain providers that will result in lower reimbursement rates.
- **Medicare Advantage payments:** Reduces reimbursement rates and imposes cost-sharing limits for Medicare's managed care plans.
- **Medicare Part A (hospital insurance):** Increases Medicare Part A tax rate for high-income earners.
- **Medicare premiums:** Reduces Medicare Part D (prescription drug) premium subsidy for high-income beneficiaries.
- **Medicare employer subsidy:** Eliminates tax deduction for employers who receive a Medicare Part D (prescription drug coverage) subsidy.
- **Disproportionate share hospital (DSH) payments:** Reduces Medicare payments to DSH hospitals. Payments may increase over time based on the percentage of uninsured served and uncompensated care provided. This feature reduces Medicaid DSH payments and requires HHS to develop a new funding formula. The effective date of the reduction was delayed until 2018, but the amount of reduction increased from $18 billion to $43 billion through 2025 (Kardish, 2015).
- **Medicaid prescription drugs:** Increases rebates that drug manufacturers give to state Medicaid programs
- **Income tax code provisions:** Increases the threshold from 7.5% to 10% of adjusted gross income to claim deduction for unreimbursed medical expenses,

prohibits purchasing over-the-counter drugs with tax-free savings accounts, increases the tax burden on distributions not used for qualified medical expenses, and limits the amount individuals may put in accounts toward medical expenses.

- **Health industry fees:** Imposes a 10% tax on indoor tanning services, 2.3% tax on all taxable medical devices, annual fees on the pharmaceutical manufacturing sector, and fees on the health insurance sector.
- **Health insurance plans:** Imposes a tax on employer-sponsored health insurance plans with aggregate expenses that exceed $10,800 for individual coverage or $29,050 for family coverage.

Although it is the responsibility of the CBO to estimate the cost of legislation as it is written, time-bound cost estimates (e.g., a 10-year estimate) have their limitations. First, the CBO must assume that all the provisions in the bill will be implemented as written. One of the most unpopular cost-saving tools—a tax on more generous health insurance plans—is not slated to take effect until 2018. Second, because the 10-year estimate, by design, does not consider costs beyond the first decade, some expected costs are not included in the estimate. Third, different methodologies may be used to calculate costs. Fourth, cost estimates cannot account for provisions that are left out of a bill. For these reasons, cost estimates should not be taken as the final word on the cost of any bill, because changes in political will can undermine the best projections.

BOX 8 Discussion Questions

The ACA includes a tax on insurers for more generous health plans. Because it is likely insurers will pass on the cost of the tax to consumers, the idea behind the tax is to provide incentives for people to choose lower-cost plans. In theory, the less money employers spend on healthcare costs (and other fringe benefits), the more they will spend on wages. The income tax paid for by workers on their higher wages will provide revenue that can be used to pay for health reform. In addition, people may be less likely to obtain unnecessary care if fewer services are covered by their plan or if cost-sharing is higher.

Is it likely that employers will trade lower benefits for higher wages? Are there times or industries where this trade-off is more or less likely to occur?

In 2017 the average cost of premiums for an employer plan was $6,690 for single coverage and $18,764 for family coverage (KFF & HRET, 2017, Section 1). Beginning in 2020, plans that exceed $10,800 for individual coverage and $29,050 for family coverage are taxed. Congress rejected lower thresholds for the tax ($8,500/$23,000) that would have raised an estimated $149 billion. Did Congress pick the right thresholds for the tax? Should they be higher or lower?

Why did Congress delay implementation of the tax until 2020? What are the pros and cons to having the tax start well after the main provisions of health reform are in place?

Sources: United States Preventive Services Taskforce. (2016, January). Breast cancer: Screening. Retrieved from https://www .uspreventiveservicestaskforce.org/Page/Document/UpdateSummaryFinal/breast-cancer-screening1?ds=1&s=breast%20 cancer; American College of Obstetricians and Gynecologists. (2016, January 11). ACOG statement on breast cancer screening guidelines. Retrieved from https://www.acog.org/About-ACOG/News-Room/Statements/2016/ACOG-Statement-on-Breast -Cancer-Screening-Guidelines; American Cancer Society (n.d.). American Cancer Society guidelines for the early detection of cancer. Retrieved July 19, 2018 from https://www.cancer.org/healthy/find-cancer-early/cancer-screening-guidelines/american -cancer-society-guidelines-for-the-early-detection-of-cancer.html

Public Health, Workforce, Prevention, and Quality

The ACA also includes a variety of programs and pilot projects that focus on improving quality of care and increasing access to preventive care. These provisions show both a commitment to these issues and the limitations of that commitment. For example, the Prevention and Public Health Fund was created to improve the nation's public health and is scheduled to provide $14 billion to support these activities from 2018 to 2027 (HHS, 2016). Congress, however, has the ability to redirect resources, and the prevention fund lost over $6 billion in 2012 when money intended for the fund was used to offset a scheduled reduction in Medicare physician payments, and it lost another $68 million in 2016 due to budget sequestration (HHS, 2017; Trust for America's Health, 2017). In addition, while task forces and pilot programs can be useful tools to try out new ideas and gather data to inform future changes, their temporary nature can also mean that progress ends once the experiment is over, especially in tight budget times. Whether these steps lead to lasting reform and needed change in the delivery of health care and in public health practice remains to be seen.

The ACA includes a wide range of quality improvement activities that fall into three main categories: evaluating new models of delivering health care, shifting reimbursement from volume to quality, and improving the overall system (Abrams et al., 2015). New models of healthcare delivery include accountable care organizations, which combine a variety of providers who collectively assume responsibility for the cost and quality of patient care, and patient-centered medical homes, which provide comprehensive and coordinated primary care. Reimbursement reforms include strategies such as penalizing hospitals with high rates of hospital-acquired infections or providing bonuses or penalties based on performance on quality measurements. Finally, overall system improvement efforts are highlighted by the National Strategy for Quality Improvement and the Patient-Centered Outcomes Research Institute (PCORI). The priorities of the National Strategy for Quality Improvement include improving delivery of healthcare services, patient outcomes, and population health. PCORI, a comparative effectiveness institute, was created to consider the clinical effectiveness of medical treatments. The idea behind comparative effectiveness is to determine which procedures, devices, and pharmaceuticals provide the best value for a given outcome. The institute is designed to supply information to help providers, patients, and others make decisions; Congress has stipulated, however, that findings from the institute may not be construed as mandates or recommendations for payment, coverage, or treatment decisions.

The ACA also provides funds to promote public health, wellness, and a stable and high-quality healthcare workforce. In addition to the Public Health and Prevention Fund, the law calls for the creation of a new regular corps and ready reserve corps to assist when public health emergencies occur. Also, a variety of programs and incentives are in place to promote employer wellness programs. Finally, the workforce shortage is addressed through graduate medical education reforms that promote primary care training; increases in scholarships and loans to support primary care providers and workforce diversity; and education, training, and loan repayment programs to address the primary care nursing shortage.

BOX 9 Discussion Questions

There is a debate about the proper age at which to start regular mammogram screenings to detect breast cancer in women who do not have specific risk factors for the disease. As of 2009, the U.S. Preventive Services Task Force recommends waiting until age 50 years to begin mammogram screening for breast cancer and further recommends that screening should occur every 2 years. It also stated, however, that the final decision about the initial timing and frequency of breast cancer screening should be made by the patient and her physician. In making its recommendations, the Task Force found that physicians would need to screen 1,000 women to save 1 woman's life and concluded that earlier and/or more frequent screening was not worth the harm associated with false positives (anxiety, unnecessary biopsies, overtreatment). Other organizations disagree with the U.S. Preventive Services Task Force and conclude that the lifesaving effects of more routine mammogram screening outweigh the potential harm. Thus, the American Cancer Society recommends having routine annual mammograms from age 45 to 54 years (or 40 if the patient so chooses) and then every 2 years thereafter. The American College of Obstetricians and Gynecologists recommends starting annual mammograms at age 40 years.

The idea of comparative effectiveness research is to provide information about the value of different tools. Once that information is available, however, who should make the decisions about whether to provide coverage and reimbursement for a particular good or service? Can one objectively assess the potential harms and benefits associated with mammograms or other services or medications? Should decisions be made solely by the patient and treating provider? Does it matter if decisions affect taxpayers (for example, if a patient is covered by a government program such as Medicare or the Veterans Administration)?

▶ The U.S. Supreme Court's Decision in the Case of *National Federation of Independent Business v. Sebelius*

In November 2011, in the first of what would be several ACA-related decisions, the U.S. Supreme Court agreed to decide four issues related to the legality of the ACA, two of which remain relevant for purposes of this text: (1) whether Congress had the power under the federal Constitution to enact the individual insurance coverage requirement and (2) whether it was unconstitutionally coercive for Congress, through the ACA, to threaten to take away existing federal Medicaid funding from states that did not want to implement the Medicaid expansion.

In June of the following year, the court handed down a remarkable 5–4 decision in the case of *National Federation of Independent Business, et al., v. Sebelius, Secretary of Health and Human Services, et al.* The opinion was surprising for two reasons: it defied expectation—few people thought that the entirety of the ACA would be found constitutional by a majority of the court—and Chief Justice Roberts, a conservative, ended up in the majority with the court's relatively liberal members (Justices Ginsburg, Breyer, Sotomayor, and Kagan).

The court first tackled the question of whether Congress exceeded its authority in effectively forcing most everyone to carry health insurance. It concluded, not totally unexpectedly given the outcome of the court's more recent Commerce Clause decisions (*United States v. Lopez*, 1995), that the "individual mandate" amounted to an unconstitutional reach on the part of federal legislators:

> The individual mandate . . . does not regulate existing commercial activity. It instead compels individuals to become active in commerce by purchasing a product, on the ground that their failure to do so affects interstate commerce. Construing the commerce clause to permit congress to regulate individuals precisely because they are doing nothing would open a new and potentially vast domain to congressional authority. (*NFIB*, 2012, p. 2587)

Surprisingly, however, the court's analysis of the constitutionality of the individual mandate did not end there. The court majority pivoted to Congress's power to tax, and ruled that under this separate power, the individual mandate passed constitutional muster. The court wrote:

> The exaction the Affordable Care Act imposes on those without health insurance [i.e., the financial penalty assessed on those who do not obtain minimum health insurance coverage] looks like a tax in many respects.... In distinguishing penalties from taxes, this Court has explained that "if the concept of penalty means anything, it means punishment for an unlawful actor omission." While the individual mandate clearly aims to induce the purchase of health insurance, it need not be read to declare that failing to do so is unlawful. Neither the Act nor any other law attaches negative legal consequences to not buying health insurance, beyond requiring a payment to the IRS. (*NFIB*, 2012, p. 2595)

Read together, the Supreme Court's analysis of the individual mandate under the Commerce Clause and the Taxing and Spending Clause leads to the following conclusion: although Congress could not outright *command* Americans to buy health insurance, it could *tax* those who choose not to.

Next, the court turned its attention to whether the ACA's Medicaid expansion was structured in a way that effectively, and unlawfully, coerced states into adopting it. Fully half of the states in the country—the 26 that sued to halt implementation of the ACA—believed the answer to be "yes." As originally passed into law, the ACA allowed the secretary of HHS to terminate *all* of a state's Medicaid funding in the event that the state failed to implement the Medicaid expansion—even those Medicaid funds that a state would receive that were unconnected to the expansion. This, the states argued, amounted to a coercively unacceptable choice: either adopt the ACA Medicaid expansion or potentially receive no federal Medicaid financing at all. As a result, they asked the court to rule that the Medicaid expansion itself was unconstitutional.

The court responded to this argument in two ways. On the one hand, it determined that the Medicaid expansion itself was perfectly constitutional; on the other hand, the court ruled that it was indeed unconstitutional for HHS to penalize states that did not adopt the expansion by terminating all Medicaid funding:

The Constitution simply does not give Congress the authority to require the States to regulate. That is true whether Congress directly commands a State to regulate or indirectly coerces a State to adopt a federal regulatory system as its own.... When, for example, such conditions take the form of threats to terminate other significant independent grants, the conditions are properly viewed as a means of pressuring the States to accept policy changes.... Nothing in our opinion precludes Congress from offering funds under the Affordable Care Act to expand the availability of health-care, and requiring that States accepting such funds comply with the conditions on their use. What Congress is not free to do is to penalize States that choose not to participate in that new program by taking away their existing Medicaid funding. (*NFIB*, 2012, pp. 2602–2607)

This twin ruling had the effect of making the ACA Medicaid expansion optional rather than mandatory, and states have been deciding individually whether to implement it. As of the time of this writing, 33 states and the District of Columbia have adopted the ACA's Medicaid expansion, while 17 states have not adopted the expansion (though note that the latter number is noticeably lower than the number of states [26] that originally argued in *NFIB v. Sebelius* that the Medicaid expansion was unconstitutionally coercive) (Advisory Board, 2018).

▶ States and Health Reform

Before the ACA and in the wake of numerous failed attempts at national health reform, states had been active players in health reform. Filling the gap left by the lack of federal action, states took steps to experiment with individual mandates, employer mandates, small business pools, and programs to reduce the number of uninsured. Although the ACA is a federal law, it is full of state obligations and opportunities for state innovation. Even though governors in many states have expressed opposition to health reform, numerous states will expend significant efforts toward continued implementation of the ACA over the next several years. States will have their hands full developing and running health insurance exchanges, regulating the private health insurance market, and implementing Medicaid changes.

The Supreme Court's decision to transform the ACA's Medicaid expansion from a mandatory program change to a state option has significant ramifications. As noted above, 33 states and the District of Columbia have chosen to expand Medicaid. As a result, by February 2017 there were 16 million more enrollees than prior to the ACA, with most new enrollment occurring in expansion states (Medicaid CHIP Payment and Access Commission, n.d.). Not surprisingly, expansion states have witnessed significant increases in Medicaid enrollment, both among newly eligible enrollees and individuals who were previously eligible but nonetheless unenrolled. This latter group is a result of the "welcome mat" or "woodwork" effect, when increases, incentives, and outreach result in more previously eligible individuals joining the program (Antonisse, Garfield, Rudowitz, & Artiga, 2018). The number of new Medicaid beneficiaries will ultimately depend on how many states eventually choose to expand their Medicaid program.

The court's decision drastically changed the blueprint of health reform. The ACA was designed assuming Medicaid expansion in every state, meaning there would be uniform coverage across the country for individuals earning below 138% of the federal poverty level. Under this plan, Medicaid would provide insurance for the lowest-income individuals, while state exchanges (with the assistance of federal subsidies) and employer-sponsored insurance would provide coverage for those who had higher earnings. It is now estimated that in states that do not expand their Medicaid program, 2.2 million people with incomes below the poverty line will remain uninsured because their incomes are too high to qualify for the state's traditional Medicaid program, yet too low to be able to afford private insurance in the exchanges because they do not qualify for subsidies (because it was assumed Medicaid would be expanded nationally, premium subsidies are available only for individuals earning at least 100% of poverty). The vast majority of them (89%) live in the South, reflecting that region's population demographics (e.g., more poor uninsured adults, higher uninsured rate) and resistance to Medicaid expansion (Garfield, Damico, & Orgera, 2018).

As noted earlier, the Trump administration's policy choices have put states at the center of health reform. The administration is providing states with a variety of tools that increase a state's ability to mold its health insurance market and Medicaid program. For example, political leaders in states that embrace more liberal positions may counter the administration's policies by using state insurance regulations to block short-term plans, implement a state-based individual mandate, and maintain a generous definition of EHBs. Discussions in some left-leaning states involve creating a public option to compete with private insurers and allowing uninsured individuals to buy into Medicaid (Brownstein, 2018). In states with more conservative leaders, it is likely that health insurance products that are not required to meet ACA requirements will flourish and that Medicaid waivers that include features such as work requirements and provisions that allow beneficiaries to be locked out for administrative reasons will be implemented (Brownstein, 2018; Quinn, 2018). As a result, the health insurance landscape is moving closer to pre-ACA days, when the cost and content of one's insurance plan depended on where one lived.

▶ Key Issues Going Forward

At the time of this writing, the Republican effort to repeal and replace the ACA has stalled. Many in the party want to keep working toward that goal, while others, including the Senate leadership, appear ready to focus on other matters. President Trump appears to support efforts to continue to reform health reform but does not any longer seem to be making it a priority. Of course, the political landscape could change dramatically after the 2018 midterm elections. If Democrats gain control of either the House or the Senate, or even gain a significant number of seats, it is unlikely Congress would pass a major reform bill. If Republicans maintain a sizeable majority in the House and pick up a few seats in the Senate, a new Congress may approve the bills that were defeated in 2017. Assuming Congress does not repeal and replace the ACA, it is unclear whether the Trump administration's executive actions will result in the ACA's "death by 1,000 cuts," or whether Congress's inability to repeal the law will eventually cement the ACA as an accepted part of the fabric that holds together our healthcare and public health systems. Until the ACA's future becomes clearer, we discuss here a few major political and implementation issues that will likely dominate the health reform discussion in the near term.

Congressional Activity

The Republicans gained control of both chambers of Congress and of the White House in the 2016 election and spent the better part of the spring and summer in 2017 wrestling with ACA repeal and replacement bills. After 7 years of campaigning on (and winning with) a platform that included repealing and replacing the ACA, Republican legislators felt a strong obligation to keep their promise. While the party was unified in its opposition to the ACA, it was less successful agreeing on a replacement plan. With a slim majority in the Senate (52 Republicans, 48 Democrats) and no Democrats supporting this effort, Republicans found it impossible to meet the demands of moderate Republicans who wanted to protect the ACA's insurance gains and conservative Republicans who wanted to eliminate as many ACA requirements, regulations, and taxes as possible. Republicans faced a similar dilemma in the House, but were able to succeed in passing a reform bill because they had a little more room for disagreement. They could tolerate 21 Republican defectors and still pass a bill without support from the Democrats. Even though Republicans were not successful in 2017 in passing a bill the House and Senate could agree on, it is worthwhile to consider the substance and politics of that debate to understand what Republicans hope to achieve when altering the ACA and how the 2018 midterm elections could affect the future of health reform.

After much political drama, including one failed vote, the House passed its ACA replacement bill, the American Health Care Act of 2017 (AHCA), on May 4, 2017 by a narrow 217–213 margin. Every Democrat and 20 Republicans voted against the bill. In the Senate, Republicans drafted the Better Care Reconciliation Act of 2017 (BCRA) as a substitution amendment to replace the AHCA. The BCRA followed the same general contours of the AHCA. After barely mustering sufficient support to proceed with debate on the bill, the Senate voted against the BCRA on July 25, 2017. All Democrats and nine Republicans opposed the bill (Fox, Lee, Mattingly, & Barrett, 2017). The next day, all Democrats and seven Republicans also voted against a bill that would have simply repealed the ACA (effective in 2 years) and did not include any type of replacement (Lee & Mattingly, 2017). This repeal-only bill actually passed Congress while President Obama was in office, but because members of Congress who voted for repeal knew that Obama would veto the bill, it was considered a protest vote more than an agreement on a policy position.

During the 2017 Senate debate, Sen. John McCain (R-AZ), who at the time had been recently diagnosed with aggressive brain cancer (and who died in late August 2018 while still a member of the Senate), provided a moment of high drama. His "no" vote was the third Republican vote (along with those of Sens. Lisa Murkowski [R-AL] and Susan Collins [R-ME]) that ultimately doomed what was referred to as the "skinny repeal" option (Fox, 2017). The skinny repeal option eliminated just the individual and employer mandates as well as a tax on medical devices. It was a bill that few actually wanted to become law, and it was projected to increase premiums and drastically reduce the number of insured individuals. Even the senators who voted for the bill did so only after assurances that the House would not pass it.

Why, then, move forward with a bill few supported? The goal was to reach a "conference committee" wherein the House and Senate could work to reach a repeal-and-replace compromise, which would then be sent back to each chamber for approval. At that point, the political pressure to support a compromise bill would have been immense. The vote for the skinny repeal bill was a vote to keep the health reform debate alive, but risked a result that few desired. In voting against this strategy, the three Republican senators who voted "no" urged their colleagues to move forward in a bipartisan manner and to follow regular order in the Senate (e.g., holding hearings, passing bills through committee).

Even though the primary legislative bills—the AHCA and BCRA—did not have sufficient support across Congress to become law, and some of their provisions may not have been allowed under reconciliation rules, it is worth considering the main features of the bills to understand the type of health reform changes many Republicans support (**TABLE 4**). Overall, these bills reduced taxes, eliminated government mandates, lowered federal government spending, lowered premiums for some

TABLE 4   Comparison of U.S. House and Senate Bills Designed to Replace the Affordable Care Act

	American Health Care Act (House)	**Better Care Reconciliation Act (Senate)**
Premium tax credits	Replaces with tax credits based on age only, not income or geographic area	Keeps tax credits, lowers eligibility to 350%, includes those under 100% FPL, tied to less expensive benchmark, changes individual contribution levels so older consumers pay more
Individual mandate	Eliminates penalties, replaces with 1-year 30% premium surcharge if lapse in coverage	Eliminates penalties, replaces with 6-month waiting period if lapse in coverage
Employer mandate	Eliminates penalties	Eliminates penalties
Medicaid expansion	Phases out at end of 2019	Phases out by end of 2024
ACA taxes	Eliminates most key taxes	Eliminates many key taxes, keeps Medicare surtax and investment tax on high-income earners
Essential health benefits	Allows state waivers to redefine	Allows state waivers to redefine

Medicaid program	Changes to block grant or per-capita allotment in 2020, allows work requirements	Changes to block grant or per-capita allotment in 2020, allows work requirements
CSR funds	Funds through 2019, repeals in 2020	Funds through 2019, repeals in 2020
Women's health services	Defunds Planned Parenthood for 1 year; redefines qualified plan to exclude plans that provide abortion services except for rape, incest, or life of mother in danger	Defunds Planned Parenthood for 1 year; redefines qualified plan to exclude plans that provide abortion services except for rape, incest, or life of mother in danger
Private market rules	Keeps guaranteed issue, dependent coverage until 26; keeps preexisting condition protection	Keeps guaranteed issue, dependent coverage until 26; keeps preexisting condition protection; permits sale of noncompliant plans as long as selling one ACA-compliant plan
State stabilization pool	Provides $123 billion over 9 years	Provides $182 billion over 9 years
Public health prevention fund	Eliminates	Eliminates
Age rating band	Changes to 5-to-1 but allows for state variation	Changes to 5-to-1 but allows for state variation
CBO estimate— uninsured	23 million more uninsured by 2026	22 million more uninsured by 2026
CBO estimate— federal savings	$119 billion	$321 billion

ACA = Affordable Care Act; CBO = Congressional Budget Office; FPL = federal poverty level.

people while increasing them for others, phased out the Medicaid expansion under the ACA, and ended Medicaid as an entitlement program. According to the CBO, the effect of the bills would be to significantly increase the number of uninsured, significantly reduce the deficit, lower costs for young and healthy consumers, and increase costs for older and poorer consumers (CBO, 2017a; CBO, 2017b).

Major industry players and a clear majority of the public opposed the proposed bills to repeal and replace the ACA. Industry groups such as hospitals, physicians, safety net providers, and insurers were concerned about the health and financial effects of the bills, while key conservative groups (e.g., Heritage Foundation, Club for Growth) did not think the bills made sufficient changes (Watkins, 2017). While 64% of respondents in one poll indicated either a preference to keep the ACA as it is or to modify it, a clear partisan divide existed (Kirzinger, DiJulio, Wu, & Brodie, 2017). Nine out of 10 Democrats supported keeping or modifying the ACA, while only 3 out of 10 Republicans agreed. Most Republicans (about 75%) indicated they wanted the ACA repealed and replaced at some point (Kahn & Erhman, 2017). For these reasons, it is not surprising that many Republican legislators feared the ramifications of disappointing their conservative base and donors by not repealing the ACA more than they feared whatever hazards awaited if they supported a bill that was unpopular with their constituencies.

One thing Congress has not tried yet is a bipartisan approach. A clear majority of the public (71%) strongly prefers for Republicans and Democrats to work together on health reform, and a number of legislators from both sides of the aisle have indicated a desire to do so (Kirzinger et al., 2017). While a partisan divide remains here as well, 41% of all Republicans and 46% of Trump supporters would like to see the parties work together (Kirzinger et al., 2017). After the failed Senate efforts, Sen. Lamar Alexander (R-TN), Chair of the Senate committee on Health, Education, Labor and Pensions, agreed to open bipartisan hearings on fixing the individual marketplace (Park, 2017). In addition, a group of bipartisan legislators from the House announced a plan to improve the ACA. Their strategy includes paying low-income CSRs to insurers, providing federal funds to the states to create reinsurance funds and other programs to lower premiums, applying the employer mandate to employers with 500 (instead of 50) or more employees, redefining full-time employee as those who work 40 hours per week, obtaining clarification from HHS about a section 1332 waiver process, and repealing the medical device tax (Lee, 2017). They also recommend offsetting the federal funds spent on these ideas, but do not indicate how current funding should be cut.

The political difficulty of repealing and replacing the ACA is not surprising. It is always difficult to take away benefits once people have started to use them. Supporting a bill that would result in over 20 million people losing insurance is clearly more politically perilous than not supporting legislation (i.e., the ACA) that would deliver health insurance to 20 million people for the first time. This is particularly true for federal legislators who hail from states that (1) implemented the ACA's Medicaid expansion and (2) have Republican governors. Why? Much of the savings from the House and Senate bills came from reduced Medicaid spending, both through the elimination of the expansion and by changing the entire program from an entitlement program to a block grant or per-capita allotment. In turn, states would either have had to absorb the federal spending reductions in their own budgets or absorb the healthcare costs of having more uninsured residents. Indeed, the proposed changes to Medicaid, which went well beyond repealing and replacing the ACA, resulted in many of the biggest criticisms from moderate Republicans. Also, Medicaid has become even more important to the nation now that it is grappling with an opioid epidemic, because Medicaid and CHIP cover approximately one-third of individuals with an opioid addiction. This is nearly double the share covered by Medicaid in 2005, and the increase is mostly due to the ACA Medicaid expansion (KFF, 2017c).

The Senate Republican leadership also made a difficult political situation even harder by alienating several of their own members when the leadership decided that the ACA repeal bills would be drafted in relative secret, ignored regular process (by not holding hearings, debates, mark-ups), used reconciliation to avoid a filibuster, and expected their members to vote on bills they had little time to review. Sen. John Cornyn (R-TX), the second-ranking Republican in the Senate, went so far as to say that knowing prior to the start of debate which bill the Republicans would be voting on was "a luxury we don't have" (Sullivan, 2017). This was a hard pill to swallow for many Republicans who vilified the Democrats for their partisan approach to passing the ACA and who mocked then-House Speaker Nancy Pelosi (D-CA) for saying, "we have to pass the healthcare bill so that you can find out what's in it" (Capehart, 2010). While ultimately Republican leaders were not successful in getting the legislation passed, they decided that the negative ramifications of these hardball tactics were easier to survive than the negative publicity of a drawn-out process where opposition groups could mobilize their resources.

Insurance Plan Premium Rates

One of the key issues to monitor going forward is the affordability of health insurance plans under the ACA. Most people were pleasantly surprised by premium rates for 2014 and 2015, although there was a lot of variation across the country. Insurers had incentive to keep premiums low because they wanted to encourage people to enroll in their health plans. In addition, there was limited information about who would be in the insurance pools that could have assisted insurers with premium rate setting, and many plans contracted with a narrower set of providers as a way to keep premiums low. After moving past the initial enrollment period, will insurance companies hike premiums in future years?

Going into 2018, insurers were faced with significant uncertainty due to the political landscape. With Congress reviewing a variety of repeal-and-replace plans and the Trump administration threatening to let ACA reforms fail, insurers did not know what to expect in the upcoming year, and uncertainty is not something that makes for a stable health insurance market. As a result, insurers asked for delays in submitting premium rates, and some even submitted two rates depending on the outcome of certain political decisions (Mangan, 2017). Many insurers submitted requests for double-digit increases. For example, insurers in Maryland asked for rate increases ranging from 18% to 60%, and in Connecticut the range was 15% to 34%. Nevada requested an average rate hike of 38%, and Colorado's request was similar, with an average increase of 41% (Livingston, 2017; Luhby, 2017a). On average, 2018 premiums were expected to increase by 17% for bronze plans, 32% for silver plans, and 18% for gold plans (Semanskee, Claxton, & Leavitt, 2017).

There is continuing uncertainty going into 2019. Insurers have to contend with the unknown effect of factors that might lead to higher costs. Primary concerns that could lead to premium increases include the individual mandate penalty repeal, the defunding of CSR payments, policy changes (e.g., expanded short-term limited duration plans) that may result in sicker marketplace pools as healthier enrollees leave plans, varying estimates of medical inflation, and changes to the ACA's risk adjustment program (Corlette, 2018). Other factors may reduce premium costs, including suspension of a tax on health insurers, reduction of the corporate tax rate for insurers, the ability to offer less generous benefits, and state policies limiting short-term plans (Corlette, 2018). Based on limited early plan filings, it is estimated that silver plan premiums will increase 15% in 2019, with wide variation across the country. For example, the average silver plan is expected to decrease by 5% in Minnesota, increase by 16% in New York, and increase by 53% in Maryland (Brantley & Brooker, 2018).

The fate of the risk adjustment program is an issue insurers are watching closely. This program was created to remove incentives for insurers to try to enroll healthy consumers over unhealthy ones. The program transfers funds from non-grandfathered plans in the small and individual market with healthier enrollees to those plans with less healthy enrollees. While states may choose to run their own risk adjustment program, none have chosen to do so at this time (Keith, 2018a). Due to conflicting court decisions regarding the risk adjustment formula, CMS suspended risk adjustment payment transfers from 2014 to 2018 (Keith, 2018a). About 3 weeks later, the Trump administration reversed course due to fears over the financial consequences for insurers. This type of uncertainty makes it difficult for insurers to establish viable operations in the health insurance market.

Reinsurance is another tool that could help insurers reduce premiums. Insurers or companies may purchase reinsurance to protect themselves against losses from high-cost enrollees—losses that would lead to premium increases for everyone in the pool (Swartz, 2017). Essentially, insurers take out a policy to protect against costs in a certain segment of an individual's coverage (e.g., costs between $100,000 and $200,000). As with most insurance, the health insurer will pay an annual premium for this reinsurance, a deductible before reinsurance takes effect, and a co-payment once the deductible is met (Swartz, 2017). Even so, it is cheaper for the insurer to pay the costs of reinsurance instead of the full cost of care for a high-risk enrollee. By keeping costs down, insurers reduce not only premiums for enrollees, but also premium tax credits paid by the federal government. For that reason, the federal government has an incentive to promote reinsurance programs. The Trump administration appears to favor reinsurance programs and sent a letter to the governors encouraging them to establish one through an ACA section 1332 State Innovation waiver (Clark, n.d.).

In the last few years, 19 states either introduced legislation to create their own reinsurance program (9 enacted) or applied for a §1332 waiver (Clark, n.d.). Section 1332 waivers allow states to finance part of the reinsurance program with a "federal pass-through" from the savings attributed to lower premiums (Clark, n.d.). As of July 2018, only Alaska, Minnesota, and Oregon have an approved waiver, with the federal government covering 97% (AK), 61% (MN), and 48% (OR) of the costs, respectively (Clark, n.d.). The programs are effective, with premium increases in Alaska dropping from 42% to 7% and premiums in Minnesota going from a 67% increase to a 15% decrease (Clark, n.d.). While these results are promising, many states cannot afford to establish a program because they have to front the entire cost and wait for the federal government to reimburse its share. The programs are indeed expensive; Minnesota's program cost $271 million and Oregon's cost $90 million (Clark, n.d.). Even if states are able to establish a program and obtain federal funding, there is always the concern whether state and federal funding will be available in future years.

In the end, the political uncertainty relating to the ACA, the various executive actions that have the potential to undermine the marketplaces, and the uncertainty surrounding ongoing litigation have created a difficult business environment for health insurance plans. There remains debate about whether the exchanges are collapsing or stabilizing in the wake of these concerns. While several analyses show a stabilizing market, continued subsidy support and increased enrollment of healthier individuals are key factors to the long-term success of the exchanges (National Academy for State Health Policy, 2018; Semanskee, Cox, & Leavitt, 2018; Zeitlin, 2017).

ACA Litigation

Legal challenges to and about the ACA have been a fixture since the law's passage in 2010; there have been countless ACA cases brought in both state and federal courts. A small handful of them even reached the U.S. Supreme Court, a rarity for a law that is relatively young. First there was the Supreme Court's decision in *NFIB v. Sebelius*, which was described earlier in this text (*NFIB v. Sebelius*, 2012). Then the court decided a case that answered whether, under a federal statute called the Religious Freedom Restoration Act (RFRA), closely held private corporations have a legal right to refuse to comply with provisions of the ACA that require them to provide certain contraceptive coverage to employees (*Burwell v. Hobby Lobby Sores, Inc.*, 2014). (A closely held corporation is one that has a limited number of shareholders; in the *Hobby Lobby* case, the plaintiffs were two private, for-profit companies owned by members of a single family—Hobby Lobby Stores [owned by Evangelical Christians] and Conestoga Wood Specialties [owned by Mennonites]). In a 5–4 decision, the court majority determined that the ACA's contraception mandate imposed a significant enough burden on the plaintiff companies' exercise of their beliefs so as to violate RFRA. Just a year later, the Supreme Court ruled that subsidies available under the ACA to help individuals and small businesses buy insurance were available whether the insurance was purchased through a state-run or federally facilitated insurance exchange (*King v. Burwell*, 2015).

Then just a year after that, the court heard a case that is an offshoot of its earlier decision in *Burwell v. Hobby Lobby* (*Zubik v. Burwell*, 2016). After the *Hobby Lobby* decision, the Obama administration offered an accommodation to religious entities that objected to the requirement to provide contraceptive coverage without cost-sharing: the religious organization could simply inform HHS of its objection and identify its insurer, at which point HHS would take responsibility for ensuring that contraceptive services are provided by the insurer without the involvement of the religious organization. The accommodation, however, was not acceptable to a number of religious entities, which filed their own RFRA lawsuits. Over time, nine federal appellate courts ruled that the accommodation did not substantially burden the entities' exercise of religion; however, one appellate court ruled the opposite way, creating a division that the Supreme Court wanted to clear up. Eventually, the Supreme Court—likely split 4–4 on the merits by this time (i.e., after Justice Scalia died and the Senate failed to hold hearings on his replacement) and hoping to spark a compromise among the litigants—remanded the cases to the lower courts without a definitive answer.

At the time of this writing, this issue is still being litigated. In October 2017, the Trump administration issued interim final rules offering any for-profit or non-profit employer or insurer that objected to contraceptives for religious reasons an absolute exemption (i.e., without the need to notify the government or insurers) from providing contraceptive coverage to its employees. However, the legality of these rules has been called into question. One federal judge held (1) that the administration unlawfully bypassed a law (the Administrative Procedure Act, or APA) requiring federal agencies to adopt rules only after notice and an opportunity for public comment and (2) that the rules were likely substantively improper as well, because they lacked sufficient clarity and a proper legal basis. A different federal judge has also found that the rules violated the APA. Appeals by the Trump administration are likely.

At the time of this writing, two other ACA-related lawsuits bear mentioning (space limitations prevent us from discussing *all* of the ongoing ACA litigation). The first is a lawsuit brought by 20 Republican-led states that effectively contends that given the repeal of the individual mandate financial penalty (discussed previously), the entire ACA must fall (*Texas v. United States*, 2018). How do Texas and their counterparts reach this conclusion? They argue that absent the monetary fine for not having health insurance, the requirement to buy insurance has no legal basis, and because the insurance mandate is central to the ACA architecture, the entire law should be thrown out.

As if the lawsuit itself was not enough of a threat to the ACA, a different type of threat emerged in June 2018 when the Trump administration alerted the federal trial court hearing the case that it would not defend the ACA in court. While politically speaking this might not seem like a big deal to most readers, this decision in fact represents a dramatic break from the executive branch's tradition of defending existing statutes. While the Justice Department's filing with the trial court acknowledges that the decision not to defend an existing law deviates from history, it contends that its decision is not unprecedented. In turn, Democratic state attorneys general from 16 states and the District of Columbia have been allowed to intervene in the case to defend the ACA. Needless to say, this case will probably be on the legal radar for the foreseeable future, given the likely appeals that will follow decisions in both the federal trial and appellate courts.

The second case worth noting is perhaps more theoretical than *Texas v. United States*, but it is interesting because it stands in stark contrast to that lawsuit. In early August 2018, four cities filed a lawsuit arguing that President Trump's attempts to undermine the ACA violate his duties under the federal Constitution (*City of Columbus v. Trump*, 2018). According to the plaintiffs, a president's obligation under Article II of the Constitution to "take Care that the laws be faithfully executed" is violated by President Trump's "sabotage" of the ACA. Plaintiffs further contend that HHS is complicit in this sabotage, and that this violates both the Administrative Procedure Act and President Trump's duty under the Constitution to ensure that laws passed by Congress are faithfully executed.

To be sure, the Constitution's "take care" clause, as it is known, is rarely invoked, much less successfully. Cases of this sort are rare because the president is granted discretion with respect to how he and his administration enforce a law, and thus drawing lines that separate "faithful" from unreasonable discretion can be extremely difficult. Nonetheless, in these incredibly politicized times, this case is also worth following.

Given these and other lawsuits (both pending and still to come), it is unlikely that the Supreme Court has cleared the ACA from its docket. However, irrespective of whether the Supreme Court hands down ACA-related cases in the future, what bears keeping in mind is that judicial decisions may continue to shape the contours of the ACA for years to come.

▶ Conclusion

After decades of trying and against the predictions of numerous experts, the United States passed a health reform law that provides insurance coverage on a more universal scale than ever before, includes protections for individuals who have been historically excluded from the insurance market, and shows a concern for improving healthcare quality and access to preventive care. From a philosophical perspective, the ACA moves America toward a society where (almost) everyone is expected to have adequate access to affordable health insurance. Under this perspective, health insurance is considered both an obligation and a right: individuals are required to obtain insurance and the government is obligated to make it affordable and accessible.

At the same time, there remains in some quarters strong philosophical and political opposition to the ACA, which continues to be challenged both legislatively and in the courts. The Republican control of both Congress and the White House, and the Trump administration's policies undermining the ACA, have created a very uncertain future for health reform. Because of this opposition and because the ACA is still not close to engendering the type of support reserved for, say, Medicare, the full story of the ACA is far from being completed.

References

Abraham, J., & Royalty, A. B. (2017, January 19). *How has the Affordable Care Act affected work and wages?* Retrieved from https://ldi.upenn.edu/brief/how-has-affordable-care-act-affected-work-and-wages

Abrams, M. K., Nuzum, R., Zezza, M. A., Ryan, J., Kiszla, J., & Guterman, S. (2015, May 7). *The Affordable Care Act's payment and delivery reforms: A progress report at five years.* Retrieved from https://www.commonwealthfund.org/publications/issue-briefs/2015/may/affordable-care-acts-payment-and-delivery-system-reforms

Advisory Board. (2018, June 8). *Where the states stand on Medicaid expansion.* Retrieved from https://www.advisory.com/daily-briefing/resources/primers/medicaidmap

Affordable Health Care for America Act of 2009, H.R. 3962, 111th Cong. (2009).

Agiesta, J. (2017, March 7). *CNN/ORC poll: Public splits on revoking individual mandate.* Retrieved from https://www.cnn.com/2017/03/07/politics/health-care-replacement-poll/index.html

American Health Care Act of 2017, H.R. 1628, 115th Cong. (2017).

American Recovery and Reinvestment Act of 2009, Pub. L. No. 111-5, 123 Stat. 115 (2009).

Antonisse, L., Garfield, R., Rudowitz, R., & Artiga, S. (2018, March 28). *The effects of Medicaid expansion under the ACA: Updated findings from a literature review.* Retrieved from https://www.kff.org/medicaid/issue-brief/the-effects-of-medicaid-expansion-under-the-aca-updated-findings-from-a-literature-review-march-2018/

Appleby, J. (2008, December 20). Health reform up in the air as economy sinks. *USA Today.* Retrieved from https://usatoday30.usatoday.com/news/health/2008-12-18-health_N.htm

Aron-Dine, A. (2017, May 30). *CBO correctly predicted historic gains under ACA.* Retrieved from https://www.cbpp.org/blog/cbo-correctly-predicted-historic-coverage-gains-under-aca

Better Care Reconciliation Act of 2017, H.R. 1628, 115th Cong. (2017).

Blake, C. H., & Adolino, J. R. (2001). The enactment of national health insurance: A Boolean analysis of twenty advanced industrial countries. *Journal of Health Politics Policy and Law, 26*(4), 670–708. doi:10.1215/03616878-26-4-679

Blendon, R. J., Altman, D. E., Benson, J. M., Brodie, M., Buhr, T., Deane, C., & Buscho, S. (2008). Voters and health reform in the 2008 presidential election. *New England Journal of Medicine, 359*(19), 2050–2062. doi:10.1056/NEJMsr0807717

Blumberg, J., Holahan, J., & Buettgens, M. (2014, May 9). *Why not just eliminate the employer mandate?* Retrieved from https://www.urban.org/research/publication/why-not-just-eliminate-employer-mandate

Blumberg, J., Holahan, J., Karpman, M., & Elmendorf, C. (2018). *Characteristics of the remaining uninsured: An update.* Retrieved from https://www.urban.org/sites/default/files/publication/98764/2001914-characteristics-of-the-remaining-uninsured-an-update_0.pdf

Blumenthal, D., & Morone, J.A. (2009). *The heart of power: Health and politics in the Oval Office.* Berkeley, CA: University of California Press.

Brantley, K., & Brooker, C. (2018, June 21). *Double-digit premium increases expected in the exchange market in 2019.* Retrieved from http://avalere.com/expertise/managed-care/insights/double-digit-premium-increases-expected-in-the-exchange-market-in-2019

Brown, C. B., & O'Connor, P. (2010, January 21). The fallout: Democrats rethinking health care bill. *Politico.* Retrieved from https://www.politico.com/story/2010/01/fallout-dems-rethinking-health-bill-031693

Brownstein, R. (2018, March 8). The health care gap between red and blue America. *The Atlantic.* Retrieved from https://www.theatlantic.com/politics/archive/2018/03/obamacare-trump/555131/

Burke, C. (2013, December 17). *Rasmussen poll: Most Americans oppose ACA's individual mandate.* Retrieved from https://www.newsmax.com/Newsfront/Obamacare-majority-oppose-Rasmussen/2013/12/17/id/542447/

Burwell v. Hobby Lobby Stores, Inc., 134 S. Ct. 2751 (2014).

Capehart, J. (2010, June 12). Pelosi defends her infamous health care remark. *The Washington Post.* Retrieved from https://www.washingtonpost.com/blogs/post-partisan/post/pelosi-defends-her-infamous-health-care-remark/2012/06/20/gJQAqch6qV_blog.html?utm_term=.566e5b909d99

Center for Consumer Information and Insurance Oversight, Centers for Medicare and Medicaid Services. (2018, April 9). *Guidance on hardship exemptions from the individual shared responsibility provision for persons experiencing limited issuer options or other circumstances.* Retrieved from https://www.cms.gov/CCIIO/Resources/Regulations-and-Guidance/Downloads/2018-Hardship-Exemption-Guidance.pdf

Center on Budget and Policy Priorities. (2018). *Sabotage watch: Tracking efforts to undermine the ACA.* Retrieved from https://www.cbpp.org/sabotage-watch-tracking-efforts-to-undermine-the-aca

Centers for Medicare and Medicaid Services. (2017, May 15). *The future of SHOP: CMS intends to allow small businesses in SHOPs using Healthcare.gov more flexibility when enrolling in healthcare coverage.* Retrieved from https://www.cms.gov/CCIIO/Resources/Regulations-and-Guidance/Downloads/The-Future-of-the-SHOP-CMS-Intends-to-Allow-Small-Businesses-in-SHOPs-Using-HealthCaregov-More-Flexibility-when-Enrolling-in-Healthcare-Coverage.pdf

City of Columbus v. Trump, No. 18-cv-2364 (2018). Retrieved from https://democracyforward.org/wp-content/uploads/2018/08/ACA-Complaint.pdf

Clark, K. (n.d.). *States return to reinsurance to stabilize ACA marketplaces.* Retrieved from https://www.lexisnexis.com/communities/state-net/b/capitol-journal/archive/2018/05/11/states-return-to-reinsurance-to-stabilize-aca-marketplaces.aspx

Cohen, J., & Balz, D. (2009, September 14). Opposition to Obama's health reform plan is high, but easing. *Washington Post.* Retrieved from http://www.washingtonpost.com/wp-dyn/content/article/2009/09/13/AR2009091302962.html

Commercial Insurance. (2012, July). *Self-insured plans under health care reform.* Retrieved from http://www.ciswv.com/CIS/media/CISMedia/Documents/Self-Insured-Plans-Under-Health-Care-Reform-070312_1.pdf

Condon, S. (2010, January 20). *Scott Brown win shakes up health care fight.* Retrieved from https://www.cbsnews.com/news/scott-brown-win-shakes-up-health-care-fight/

Congressional Budget Office. (2017a). *American Health Care Act: Cost estimate.* Retrieved from https://www.cbo.gov/system/files?file=115th-congress-2017-2018/costestimate/americanhealthcareact.pdf

Congressional Budget Office. (2017b). *Better Care Reconciliation Act of 2017: Cost estimate.* Retrieved from https://www.cbo.gov/publication/52941

Congressional Budget Office. (2017c). *Federal subsidies under the Affordable Care Act for health insurance coverage related to the expansion of Medicaid and nongroup health insurance: Tables from CBOs January 2017 baseline.* Retrieved from http://acasignups.net/sites/default/files/CBO-2017-01-healthinsurance.pdf

Congressional Budget Office. (2017d). *Repealing the individual health insurance mandate: An updated estimate.* Retrieved from https://www.cbo.gov/system/files?file=115th-congress-2017 -2018/reports/53300-individualmandate.pdf

Congressional Budget Office. (2018). *Federal subsidies for health insurance coverage for people under age 65: Tables from CBOs spring 2018 projections.* Retrieved from https://www.cbo.gov/system /files?file=2018-06/51298-2018-05-healthinsurance.pdf

Corlette, S. (2018, May 21). *The effect of federal policy: What early premium rate filings can tell us about the future of the Affordable Care Act.* Retrieved from http://chirblog.org/what-early -rate-filings-tell-us-about-future-of-aca/

Coverage of Certain Preventive Services Under the Affordable Care Act, 78 Fed. Reg. 127, 29870-29899 (July 2, 2013).

Department of Health and Human Services. (2016, December 16). *Prevention and public health fund.* Retrieved from https://www.hhs.gov/open/prevention/index.html

DiJulio, B., Kirzinger, A., Wu, B., & Brodie, M. (2017, March 2). *Data note: Americans' challenge with health care costs.* Retrieved from https://www.kff.org/health-costs/poll-finding/data -note-americans-challenges-with-health-care-costs/

Eibner, C., & Nowak, S. (2018, July 11). *The effect of eliminating the individual mandate penalty and the role of behavioral factors.* Retrieved from https://www.commonwealthfund.org/publications /fund-reports/2018/jul/eliminating-individual-mandate-penalty-behavioral-factors

Emergency Economic Stabilization Act of 2008, Pub L. No. 110-343, 122 Stat. 3765 (2008).

Employee Retirement Security Income Act of 1974, Pub. L. No. 93-406, 88 Stat. 829 (1974).

Exchange establishment standards and other related standards under the Affordable Care Act, 177 Fed. Reg. 11718, 2012

Feder, J. (2004). Crowd-out and the politics of health reform. *Journal of Law, Medicine, and Ethics, 32*(3), 461-464. doi:10.1111/j.1748-720X.2004.tb00158.x

Fise, P. (2017, June 8). *Cost sharing reduction subsidies: What happens if they aren't paid?* Retrieved from https://bipartisanpolicy.org/blog/cost-sharing-reduction-subsidies-what-happens-if -they-arent-paid/

Fox, L. (2017, July 28). *John McCain's maverick moment.* Retrieved from https://www.cnn.com /2017/07/28/politics/john-mccain-maverick-health-care/index.html

Fox, L., Lee, M. J., Mattingly, P., & Barrett, T. (2017, July 26). *Senate rejects proposals to repeal and replace Obamacare.* Retrieved from http://cnnphilippines.com/world/2017/07/26/senate -rejects-proposal-to-repeal-and-replace-obamacare.html

Galewitz, P. (n.d.). *HHS targets young adults for Obamacare enrollment.* Retrieved from https://www.webmd.com/health-insurance/news/20160621/hhs-targets-young-adults-in -2017-obamacare-enrollment-plan

Garfield, R., Damico, A., & Orgera, K. (2018, June 12). *The coverage gap: Uninsured poor adults in states that do not expand Medicaid.* Retrieved from https://www.kff.org/medicaid/issue-brief /the-coverage-gap-uninsured-poor-adults-in-states-that-do-not-expand-medicaid/

Garrett, T. A. (2011, October 19). *State balanced-budget and debt rules.* Retrieved from https://files .stlouisfed.org/files/htdocs/publications/es/11/ES1133.pdf

Giovannelli, J., Lucia, K. W., Corlette, S. (2014, October 31). *Implementing the Affordable Care Act: Revisiting the ACA's essential health benefits requirements.* Retrieved from https://www.commonwealthfund.org/publications/issue-briefs/2014/oct/implementing -affordable-care-act-revisiting-acas-essential

Giovannelli, J., Volk, J., Lucia, K. W., Williams, A., & Connor K. (2015, October 27). *States revisit insurer benefit requirements, but have little data on consumers' experiences.* Retrieved from https://www.commonwealthfund.org/blog/2015/states-revisit-insurer-benefit-requirements -have-little-data-consumers-experiences

Gonzales v. Raich, 545 U.S. 1 (2005).

Gordon, C. (2003). *Dead on arrival: The politics of health care in twentieth-century America.* Princeton, NJ: Princeton University Press.

Graham, D. A. (2017, July 28). "As I have always said": Trump's ever-changing positions on health care. *The Atlantic.* Retrieved from https://www.theatlantic.com/politics/archive/2017/07 /as-i-have-always-said-trumps-ever-changing-position-on-health-care/535293/

Guttmacher Institute. (n.d.). *Abortion: Insurance coverage.* Retrieved from https://www.guttmacher .org/united-states/abortion/insurance-coverage

Guttmacher Institute. (2018a, June 1). *An overview of abortion laws*. Retrieved from https://www
.guttmacher.org/state-policy/explore/overview-abortion-laws

Guttmacher Institute. (2018b, June 11). *Insurance coverage of contraceptives*. Retrieved from https://
www.guttmacher.org/state-policy/explore/insurance-coverage-contraceptives

Hamel, L., Firth, J., & Brodie, M. (2014, April 29). *Kaiser health tracking poll—April 2014*. Retrieved
from https://www.kff.org/health-reform/poll-finding/kaiser-health-tracking-poll-april-2014/

Health Insurance Issuers Implementing Medical Loss Ratio Requirements Under the Patient
Protection and Affordable Care Act, 75 Fed. Reg. 74864 (2010).

Health Insurance Premium Tax Credit, 77 Fed. Reg., 30377 (2012, May 23).

Healthcare.gov. (n.d.). *Grandfathered health insurance plans*. Retrieved from https://www.healthcare
.gov/health-care-law-protections/grandfathered-plans/

Heart of Atlanta Motel, Inc. v. United States, 379 U.S. 241 (1964).

HHS Notice of Benefit and Payment Parameters for 2019. 83 Fed. Reg. 74, 16930-17071 (2018, April 17).

Jones, J. M. (2010, October 26). *Economy top issue for voters: Size of gov't may be more pivotal*.
Retrieved from https://news.gallup.com/poll/144029/economy-top-issue-voters-size-gov-may
-pivotal.aspx

Jost, T. S. (2004). Why can't we do what they do? National health reform abroad. *Journal of Law,
Medicine, and Ethics, 32*(3), 433–441. doi:10.1111/j.1748-720X.2004.tb00154

Jost, T. S. (2013). *Implementing health reform: Exemptions from the individual mandate*. Retrieved
from https://www.healthaffairs.org/do/10.1377/hblog20130627.032474/full/

Jost, T. S (2016, January 26). *CBO lowers marketplace enrollment predictions, increases Medicaid
growth projections (updated)*. Retrieved from https://www-healthaffairs-org.proxygw.wrlc.org
/do/10.1377/hblog20160126.052850/full/

Jost, T. S. (2017, May 15). *CMS announces plans to effectively end the SHOP exchange*. Retrieved from
https://www.healthaffairs.org/do/10.1377/hblog20170515.060112/full/

Kahn, H. (2010, January 22). Health care bill aftermath: Rep. Patrick Kennedy hails dad's dream;
Sen. John McCain sees heavy price. *ABC News*. Retrieved from https://abcnews.go.com/GMA
/HealthCare/health-care-congress-passes-landmark-reform-obama-sign/story?id=10167139

Kahn, C., & Erman, M. (2017, July 29). Exclusive: Majority of Americans want Congress to
move on from health reform. *Reuters*. Retrieved from https://www.reuters.com/article
/us-usa-healthcare-poll-idUSKBN1AE0RY

Kaiser Family Foundation. (n.d.) *Health reform FAQs*. Retrieved from https://www.kff.org
/health-reform/faq/health-reform-frequently-asked-questions/#question-who-is-eligible-for
-marketplace-premium-tax-credits

Kaiser Family Foundation. (2008). *Findings of Kaiser health tracking poll: Election 2008—October
2008*. Retrieved from https://www.kff.org/health-reform/poll-finding/findings-of-kaiser-health
-tracking-poll-election/

Kaiser Family Foundation. (2009a). *Chartpack: Kaiser health tracking poll: November 2009*. Retrieved
from https://www.kff.org/health-costs/poll-finding/chartpack-kaiser-health-tracking-poll
-november-2009/

Kaiser Family Foundation. (2009b). *Kaiser health tracking poll: August 2009*. Retrieved from https://
www.kff.org/health-costs/poll-finding/kaiser-health-tracking-poll-august-2009/

Kaiser Family Foundation. (2009c). *Key findings: Kaiser health tracking poll—September 2009*.
Retrieved from https://www.kff.org/health-costs/poll-finding/key-findings-kaiser-health
-tracking-poll-september/

Kaiser Family Foundation. (2017a, August 18). *Counties at risk for having no insurer on marketplace
(Exchange) in 2018*. Retrieved from https://www.kff.org/interactive/counties-at-risk-of
-having-no-insurer-on-the-marketplace-exchange-in-2018/

Kaiser Family Foundation. (2017b). *Kaiser health tracking poll—June 2017: ACA, replacement
plan, and Medicaid*. Retrieved from https://www.kff.org/health-reform/poll-finding/kaiser
-health-tracking-poll-june-2017-aca-replacement-plan-and-medicaid/

Kaiser Family Foundation. (2017c). *The opioid epidemic and Medicaid's role in treatment:
A look at changes over time*. Retrieved from https://www.kff.org/slideshow/the-opioid
-epidemic-and-medicaids-role-in-treatment-a-look-at-changes-over-time/

Kaiser Family Foundation. (2018). *State health insurance marketplace types, 2018*. Retrieved
from   https://www.kff.org/health-reform/state-indicator/state-health-insurance-marketplace

-types/?currentTimeframe=0&sortModel=%7B%22colId%22:%22Location%22,%22sort%22: %22asc%22%7D

Kaiser Family Foundation and Health Research Educational Trust. (2017, September 19). *2017 Employer health benefit survey.* Retrieved from https://www.kff.org/health-costs /report/2017-employer-health-benefits-survey/

Kamal,R.,Semanskee,A.,Long,M.,Claxton,G.,&Leavitt,L.(2017,October27).*Howthelossofcostsharing subsidy payments is affecting 2018 premiums.* Retrieved from https://www.kff.org/health-reform /issue-brief/how-the-loss-of-cost-sharing-subsidy-payments-is-affecting-2018-premiums/

Kardish, C. (2015, April 17). *Medicare deal delays but deepens hospital cuts.* Retrieved from http:// www.governing.com/topics/health-human-services/gov-medicare-deal-delays-hospital -cuts.html

Keith, K. (2017, October 31). *Proposed 2019 Affordable Care Act payment rules: A big role for states.* Retrieved from http://chirblog.org/proposed-2019-affordable-care-act-payment-rule-big -role-states/

Keith, K. (2018a, July 17). *ACA round up: New risk adjustment guidance, New Jersey 1332 application, GAO report on Association Health Plans.* Retrieved from https://www.healthaffairs.org/do /10.1377/hblog20180717.450336/full/

Keith, K. (2018b, April 10). *New guidance on exemptions from the individual mandate.* Retrieved from https://www.healthaffairs.org/do/10.1377/hblog20180410.721972/full/

Keith, K. (2018c, July 19). *States' lawsuit over cost-sharing reductions is dismissed.* Retrieved from https://www.healthaffairs.org/do/10.1377/hblog20180719.822849/full/

Keith, K. (2018d, April 11). *Unpacking the 2019 final payment notice (part 2).* Retrieved from https://www.healthaffairs.org/do/10.1377/hblog20180411.618457/full/

Kiley, J. (2017, June 23). *Public support for "single payer" health coverage grows, driven by Democrats.* Retrieved from http://www.pnhp.org/news/2017/june/new-gallup-and-pew-surveys-show -concern-and-hope-for-health-care

King v. Burwell, 135 S. Ct. 2480 (2015).

Kirzinger, A., DiJulio, B., Wu, B., & Brodie, M. (2017, July 14). *Kaiser health tracking poll—July 2017: What next for Republican ACA repeal and replacement plan efforts?* Retrieved from https://www .kff.org/health-reform/poll-finding/kaiser-health-tracking-poll-july-2017-whats-next-for -republican-aca-repeal-and-replacement-plan-efforts/

Kondick, K., & Skelley, G. (2016, December 15). *Incumbent re-election rates higher than average in 2016.* Retrieved from http://www.rasmussenreports.com/public_content/political_commentary /commentary_by_kyle_kondik/incumbent_reelection_rates_higher_than_average_in_2016

Kornreich, L. (2007, September 21). *Obama talks about mother's cancer battle in ad.* Retrieved from http://politicalticker.blogs.cnn.com/2007/09/21/obama-talks-about-mothers-cancer-battle -in-ad/

Lee, M. (2017, July 31). *Bipartisan coalition looks to solve problem of individual market.* Retrieved from http://www.modernhealthcare.com/article/20170731/NEWS/170739986

Lee, M. J., & Mattingly, P. (2017, July 26). *Health care debate: Senate rejects full Obamacare repeal without replacement.* Retrieved from http://www.wowt.com/content/news/Health-care-debate -Senate-rejects-full-Obamacare-repeal-without-replacement-436817863.html

Liptak, K., Luhby, T., & Mattingly, P. (2017, October 13). *Trump will end health care cost sharing subsidies.* Retrieved from https://www.cnn.com/2017/10/12/politics/obamacare-subsidies /index.html

Livingston, S. (2017, May 10). *Health insurers proposed 2018 rate hikes are early warning signs.* Retrieved from http://www.modernhealthcare.com/article/20170510/NEWS/170519999/

Luhby, T. (2017a, July 29). *Repeal is dead (for now). But will Obamacare survive?* Retrieved from https://money.cnn.com/2017/07/29/news/economy/obamacare-repeal/index.html

Luhby, T. (2017b, March 12). *What CBO got right—and wrong—on Obamacare.* Retrieved from https://money.cnn.com/2017/03/09/news/economy/cbo-obamacare/index.html

Magness, J. (2017, March 30). *America's opposition to repealing Obamacare grows, particularly among Republicans.* Retrieved from https://www.mcclatchydc.com/news/politics-government /article141562849.html

Mangan, D. (2017, April 28). *California will allow insurers to file two sets of rates: One for "Trumpcare" the other for "Obamacare."* Retrieved from https://www.cnbc.com/2017/04/28

/california-will-allow-health-insurers-to-file-two-sets-of-rates-one-for-trumpcare-other-for
-obamacare.html

Medicaid, CHIP Payment and Access Commission. (n.d.). *Medicaid enrollment changes following the ACA.* Retrieved from https://www.macpac.gov/subtopic/medicaid-enrollment
-changes-following-the-aca/

Mills, D. (2016, June 29). *Young adults targeted in this fall's Obamacare enrollment drive.* Retrieved from https://www.healthline.com/health-news/young-adults-targeted-in-obamacare-drive

Morone, J. A. (2010). Presidents and health reform: From Franklin D. Roosevelt to Barack Obama. *Health Affairs 29*(6), 1096–1100. doi:10.1377/hlthaff.2010.0420

Murray, S., & Kane, P. (2010, January 22). Pelosi: House won't pass Senate bill to save health-care reform. *Washington Post.* Retrieved from http://www.washingtonpost.com/wp-dyn/content
/article/2010/01/21/AR2010012101604.html

National Academy for State Health Policy. (2018, February 7). *Individual marketplace enrollment remains stable in the face of national uncertainty.* Retrieved from https://nashp.org
/individual-marketplace-enrollment-remains-stable-in-the-face-of-national-uncertainty/

National Archives and Record Administration. (n.d.). *Historical election results: Electoral college box scores 2000–2016.* Retrieved from https://www.archives.gov/federal-register/electoral-college
/scores2.html

National Conference of State Legislators. (2016, June 17). *States with effective rate review programs.* Retrieved from http://www.ncsl.org/research/health/health-insurance-rate-approval
-disapproval.aspx

National Federation of Independent Business v. Sebelius, 132 S. Ct. 2566 (2012).

Newport, F. (2010, November 18). U.S. still split on whether gov't should ensure healthcare. *Gallup.* Retrieved from https://news.gallup.com/poll/144839/Split-Whether-Gov-Ensure-Healthcare.
aspx

Oberlander, J. (2010). Long time coming: Why health reform finally passed. *Health Affairs, 29*(6), 1112–1116. doi:10.1377/hlthaff.2010.0447

Office of Assistant Secretary for Planning and Evaluation. (2018). *HHS poverty guidelines for 2018.* Retrieved from https://aspe.hhs.gov/poverty-guidelines

Park, M. (2017, August 2). *Senator announces bipartisan hearing on Obamacare.* Retrieved from https://www.cnn.com/2017/08/02/politics/senate-health-care-hearing-bipartisan/index.html

Patient Protection and Affordable Care Act of 2010, 42 U.S.C. § 18001 (2010).

Pear, R. (2017, June 1). Trump rule could deny birth control coverage to hundreds of thousands of women. *The New York Times.* Retrieved from https://www.nytimes.com/2017/06/01/us
/politics/birth-control-women-trump-health-care.html

Pollitz, K., Long, M., Semanskee, A., & Kamal, R. (2018, April 23). *Understanding short-term limited duration health insurance.* Retrieved from https://www.kff.org/health-reform/issue-brief
/understanding-short-term-limited-duration-health-insurance/

Quinn, M. (2018, April 12). *Trump's new Obamacare rules give states more power. Will they take it?* Retrieved from http://www.governing.com/topics/health-human-services/gov-trump
-obamacare-states.html

Rosenbaum, S., Teitelbaum, J., & Hayes, K. (2011). Crossing the Rubicon: The impact of the Affordable Care Act on the content of insurance coverage for persons with disabilities. *Notre Dame Journal of Law, Ethics, and Public Policy, 25*(2), 527–562. Retrieved from https://
scholarship.law.nd.edu/ndjlepp/vol25/iss2/16

Saad, L. (2008, November 10). Obama and Bush: A contrast in popularity. *Gallup.* Retrieved from https://news.gallup.com/poll/111838/obama-bush-contrast-popularity.aspx

Scott, D. (2018, April 13). *A requiem for the individual mandate.* Retrieved from https://
www.vox.com/policy-and-politics/2018/4/13/17226566/obamacare-penalty-2018
-individual-mandate-still-in-effect

Semanskee, A., Claxton, G., & Leavitt, L. (2017, November 29). *How premiums are changing in 2018.* Retrieved from https://www.kff.org/health-reform/issue-brief/how-premiums-are-changing
-in-2018/

Semanskee, A., Cox, C., & Leavitt, L. (2018, June 26). *Individual insurance market performance in 2018.* Retrieved from https://www.kff.org/private-insurance/issue-brief/individual-insurance
-market-performance-in-early-2018/